Green Div

GREENHOUSE GARDENING FOR BEGINNERS

THE STEP BY STEP GUIDE TO BUILD A YEAR ROUND SOLAR GREEN-HOUSE AND GROW HERBS, ORGANIC FRUITS AND VEGETABLES, PLANTTS, AND FLOWERS.

NO PRIOR EXPERIENCE REQUIREND

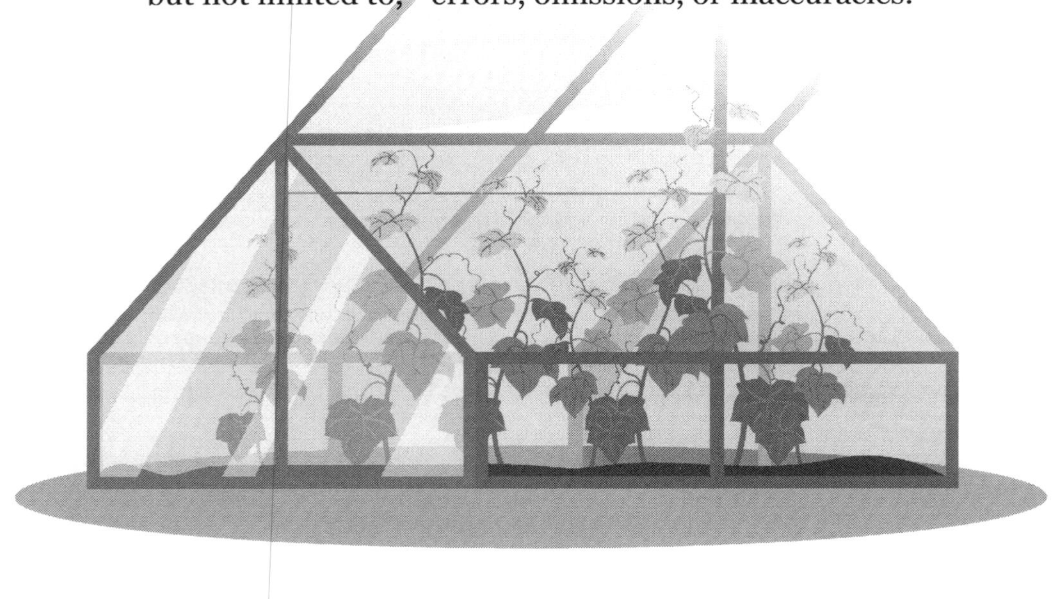

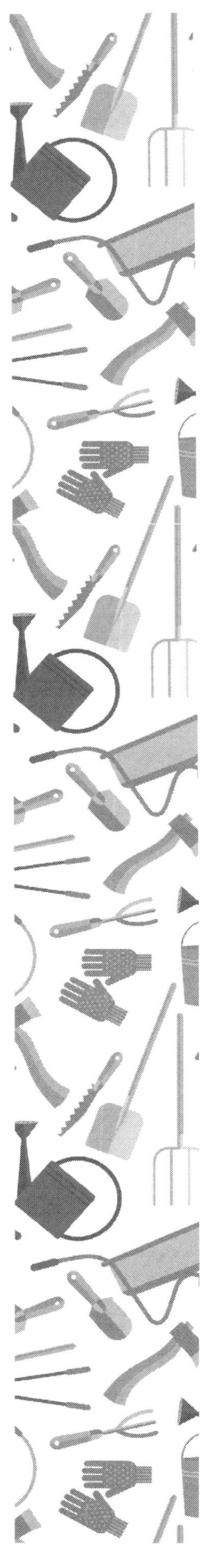

TABLE OF CONTENTS

INTRODUCTION

While many winter climates do not encourage plant production, there is an alternative for people who want to garden all year long. Greenhouses have become more and more popular, and greenhouse gardening gives budding gardeners numerous benefits.

The most significant advantage of having a greenhouse is that it can prolong the growing season. When the soil and outside temperatures are too harsh to grow in the winter months, a greenhouse can be sufficiently warm to sustain several different flowers and vegetables.

Greenhouse gardening is such an exciting experience, especially if you love growing and nurturing plants. When you set up a greenhouse, you will provide plants with everything they need to grow and thrive. Setting up the most optimal environment will help them grow better, and you will be rewarded with a beautiful harvest.

Greenhouse gardening can also help save you money after the initial investment. By allowing your fruits and vegetables to grow longer each year, greenhouses will enable you to spend less on your local grocery shop's fruits and vegetables. A good way to grow within a greenhouse is to use it mainly for overwintering plants that are not hardy in your field and take advantage of natural light beginning in mid-winter. This solution requires minimum heat extra heat and no external illumination.

As exciting as the idea sounds, there is more to setting up a greenhouse than to build a structure and put plants in it. Have you ever heard the statement, "Anything worth doing is worth doing well?" This statement is a genuine reflection of the kind of effort you should put into your greenhouse gardening project.

Many people want to experience the joy of having a greenhouse, but they are overwhelmed because they don't know how to start, or they have tried and got discouraged because they couldn't get it right. If that sounds like you, don't despair! You will avoid some of the challenges other beginners face when buying or building a greenhouse and developing, maintaining, and sustaining it for a long term.

When you set up your greenhouse, indoor growing conditions must be established that mimic growing outdoor conditions in more temperate climates. This involves ensuring air conditioning and having the nutrients the plants need.

You will start by carefully choosing your greenhouse location. "Look over a year for the sun and shadow. Find or establish a level site that gets no shade from trees or buildings. It is good to turn your greenhouse east to west for a strong southern exposure so the sun can illuminate the house all day and make the most of winter heat. Throughout the day, a brick, stone, or concrete floor retains heat from the sun and emits it during the night.

Access to water and power is another factor in the choice of locations. For seed starting, natural light levels happily begin to increase about the same time you can begin to start your seeds. Greenhouses act as a barrier between nature and what you grow, thus prolonging and potentially enhancing growing seasons.

Committing to embark on a greenhouse adventure is a serious matter. Most people consider greenhouses as an investment, which they are, due to the cost and effort required to construct and maintain one successfully.

Chapter - 1
GARDENING IS A REWARDING HOBBY

If you don't already know, a greenhouse hobby is nothing more than a small or even an enormous structure, home to fruits, vegetables, and flowers, all of which have been grown recreationally.

This type of greenhouse will be much more manageable in terms of scope and size, in sharp contrast to commercial and large-scale greenhouses. Therefore, it is firmly intended for an amateur gardener seeking to expand his or her gardening hobby. Let's look at the 15 reasons for having such a greenhouse now.

Such a greenhouse would allow you to either save your plants in the winter or reuse them in the year.

Another incentive to own a hobby greenhouse is to have fresh veggies throughout the year. This can mean the difference between harvesting and having your final tomato all year round in the fall!

When you have your greenhouse, you can extend the types of plants you produce. You see, in it, you can grow tropical plants that do not naturally grow where you live.

Getting this sort of greenhouse enables you to indulge more months of the year in your gardening hobby. You will be forced to stop gardening without a hobby glasshouse once the weather gets colder.

For plants as well, you can save a lot of money. Theoretically, a glasshouse helps you to produce as many seeds as you want. This is better than spending a lot of money on new plants when the spring finally rolls around!

Believe it or not, you can also start your own greenhouse company. By doing some market research to find out what plants are suitable in your area, you may be able to sell them to roadside stands, farmer markets, and even grocery stores.

Why do people love greenhouse gardening? We just do that because it relieves their pain! A greenhouse's environment is very relaxing, meaning your stress levels can drop just because you're in this environment.

Through your greenhouse hobby, you can even start making friends! Just share your greenhouse growing space with some of your neighbors or friends and watch the bonds of acquaintance that begin to form.

Such greenhouses are designed to last as well. It is fair for you to expect it to last for many years when you buy one (although you can also it create yourself). Several people have been using theirs with no problems for ten years or even more.

It's also possible to build your greenhouse for your hobby. Because you are someone who likes to work with his or her hands, you can even have fun creating a conservatory for your hobby even before you start enjoying all the plants you're going to grow there.

If you own an energy-efficient greenhouse, you can even help the environment. You see, such a greenhouse hobby comes with features like covers that allow the light to spread so it can illuminate across your whole greenhouse.

You may notice a boost in your health, especially if you grow your veggies in your greenhouse. Eating more fresh veggies is part of a healthy diet that is good for your health.

If you're a gardener who's always frustrated with insects beginning to kill and consume your plants, then getting your hobby greenhouse is the best option you can think of. A greenhouse hobby can protect your plants from insect pestilence.

Many people who own their greenhouse hobby say that their plants are growing faster than ever! Since you're a person who loves plants to grow, you certainly don't want to wait for them to grow forever.

The ultimate reason to own such a glasshouse is that you will enjoy a longer lifespan for the plants you grow. This is only fair when you consider that such plants are covered by a hobby greenhouse from nature's harsh conditions and the outdoors. As a result, your plants can enjoy growing strong and flourishing without the elements threatening them.

Chapter - 2
GREENHOUSE CONSTRUCTION

Site selection and foundation are not as crucial in constructing most greenhouses as constructing other buildings. Even if there is no foundation, certain factors must be considered in site selection with even the simplest greenhouse.

More importantly, moving from east to west describes a path low in the southern sky during the winter. It passes much more nearly overhead in summer, reaching its highest point on or about June 21, but it still describes an arc through the southern sky. (In the Southern Hemisphere, for the south, read north, and vice versa.)

These facts are crucially important in locating a solar home or an attached greenhouse; curiously, they are almost no important in sitting an unattached greenhouse. Solar houses and attached greenhouses must be carefully oriented toward the sun. They have all their glazing on the south side; the north side is usually opaque and heavily insulated.

WORKING WITH CONCRETE

It is much easier for the novice to lay up a concrete block foundation than to construct and lock forms and pour concrete into them. Even if you use concrete blocks, you'll have to pour footings, so you'll need to know something about concrete. What the layman calls cement, the builder calls concrete. Concrete is made by mixing water, portland cement (a powdered glue), and sand or gravel, called aggregate by builders. A mortar mix, to lay brick or block, also includes lime.

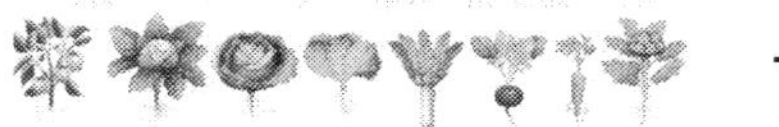

FOOTINGS

Footings are sprawling lumps (huge ones) of concrete poured below the frost line. The entire building rests on them. To make them, dig down well below the frost line in your area. Make the trench at least twice as wide as the wall atop it will be and broader than that at the corners.

Mix up the dry ingredients; the right proportion is one part cement, two parts sand, and three parts gravel. Mix them very thoroughly. Old resources tell you to do this in a wheelbarrow with a hoe. If you try this once, you will forever go to the local "We Rent Everything" place and rent a tiny portable cement mixer, no matter what they charge.

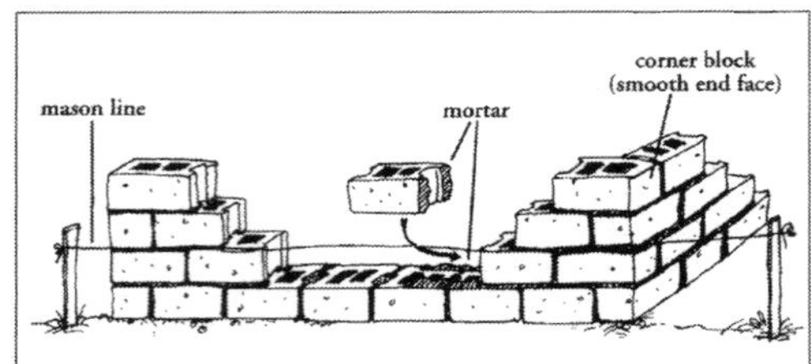

Fig. 2. A line is used to keep concrete blocks level and true as they are laid. The corner blocks are laid first; a mason's level is used to ensure that they are level and at the same height. Then a mason line is stretched from corner to corner.

WATERPROOFING AND FLASHING

Whether you build the wall yourself or have it made, it is mandatory to waterproof it by spreading a black, tarry substance all over the outside with long-handled brushes after the concrete is thoroughly dry. The contractor, if any, will gladly leave this job to you. Wear clothes you can burn afterward.

In construction, there is always another step to take. After the foundation walls are coated and covered with insulation, the excavation should be backfilled as soon as possible. Don't work on the framing until this has been done. A worker can fall about twice as far and land in a nasty position if there is a deep trench all around the building. I once did, and I wound up in the hospital.

It is customary to apply aluminum flashing over the top of a foundation wall before a wooden fence is erected. Aluminum can be bought in a long roll of the width desired, unrolled, and bent into an L shape (in the cross). It is easier to turn it over a 2x8 or something of the sort than to do it freehand. Usually, aluminum can be bent readily with the fingers, but sometimes a rubber hammer comes in handy. After it is applied, a plank can be laid to hold it until the framing is built on top of it.

Flashing serves at least three purposes: It deflects rain and snowmelt away from the wall, it serves as an insect barrier, and it helps to hold Styrofoam insulation in place.

FRAMING

The framing of a greenhouse is the support system that goes above the foundation and supports the walls and roof, whether they are totally glazed or partially opaque. The majority of owner-built greenhouses have framing made of either plastic (PVC) plumbing pipe or lumber. Greenhouses purchased as a kit from a manufacturer often use aluminum tubing; rarely, owner-builders have a supply of old-fashioned galvanized steel pipe and use that.

Often, the choice of framing depends on the skills of the builder. Someone who is experienced in putting together PVC pipe, like a plumber, will choose that. Most handymen of either sex feel more competent banging nails into wood, although PVC pipe is probably easier to work with.

Which glazing material is chosen will do a great deal to determine the framing material. Generally, when the glazing is very light, such as 6-mil plastic, the frame will be a plastic pipe or aluminum tubing. Glass, plexiglass, and other heavier materials usually rest on a wooden framework. There are examples in part III of thin, transparent plastic supported by wood. There are no examples of glass supported by PVC pipe, nor have I ever seen such a structure.

Most people who would consider building their greenhouses have some idea of building a simple frame structure, such as a doghouse (fig. 3). To create a greenhouse, just make an oversized doghouse and cover it with a transparent material. Most doghouses use a simple modification of modern platform-framing construction.

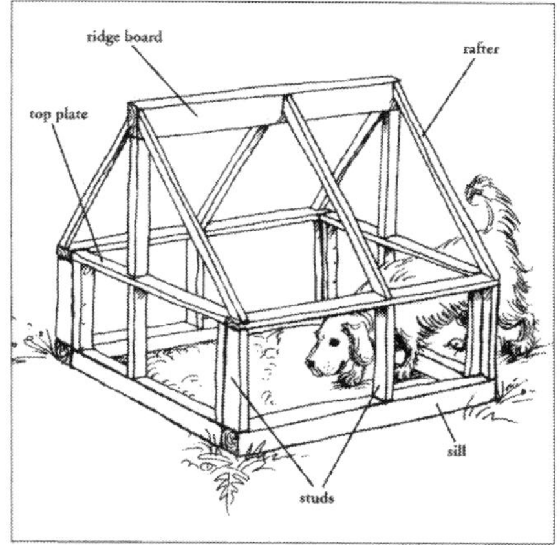

Fig. 3. A doghouse is like any wood-framed building, in miniature: It has sills, studs, top plates, rafters, and a ridge board.

FRAMING WINDOW AND DOOR OPENINGS

Many greenhouses don't have windows; they are nothing but windows. However, all greenhouses have a door or doors, and some have windows, especially in the ends. Whether you are framing an opening in a wall for a door or window, in a roof for a skylight or chimney, or in a wooden floor, the technique is the same: you frame the opening with double members to compensate for creating a weakness in the structure. What makes this confusing for the layman is that the terminology varies slightly from floors to walls to roofs_ I will describe here how to frame a window opening, then point out any differences between this and a door or other space.

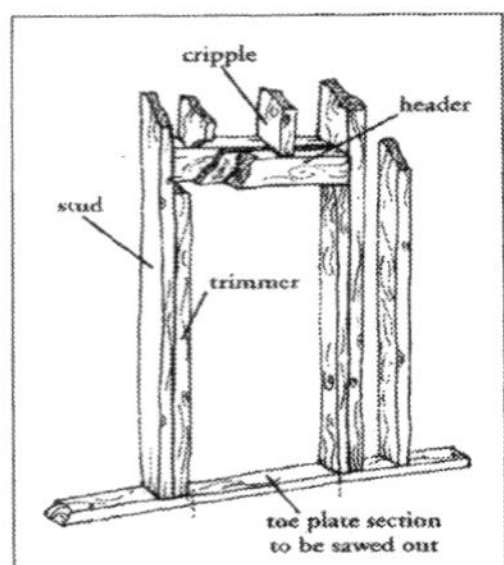

Fig. 5. The rough opening for a door is like that for a window, except that when the door is ready to be mounted, the rough sill (a portion of the toe plate) must be sawed out.

Doors are framed exactly like windows, with one exception: Since the bottom of the door will, presumably, be at the level of the final, finished floor, plan accordingly. There is no rough sill, but prepare the rough opening so that when you saw out the part of the toe plate at the bottom of the door opening, the rough start will be exactly the right size. Sawing this is a nuisance because it can't be done with an ordinary power saw. It must be done by hand or with a unique power tool.

If any holes for skylights, the most common mistake you will probably make once is to forget that the rough opening must be the right size after the trimmers are added. The distance between the two original studs has to be 3 inches greater than the RO's width.

FRAMING THE ROOF

When the walls are in place, build the roof. For a freestanding greenhouse, you will be making the usual kind of roof, with both sides sloping to a ridge or peak. However, most attached greenhouses have **shed roofs,** which are easier to build since the rafters simply slope from a low side to a high side, where they intersect the house wall.

Put rafters on each end at the appropriate angle, and cut **birdsmouths** into them, if necessary. Birdsmouth is the poetic term carpenters use for a triangular bite taken out of a rafter near its lower end so that it will seat itself into the top plate a few inches. This is done when the roof is overhang. Most greenhouse builders desire a certain amount of overhang. If the roof slopes to the south, the most common arrangement in

attached greenhouses, and is not too steep, an overhang of about a foot will allow winter sun to shine in the windows and block out the summer sun. Besides, a substantial overhang keeps rain and snowmelt off walls and windows.

You can figure out the exact angles and positions of the cuts you need with graph paper, a rafter square, and trigonometry. (The courtyard of the hypotenuse equals the sum of the courts of the other two sides. The rafter is the hypotenuse.) However, the easiest way is to find a large, flat, dry surface, like a barn floor, and layout a full-scale model, using an actual rafter and actual pieces of lumber to represent top plates, ridge boards, or whatever you need.

FINISH MATERIALS

Most greenhouse walls and roofs will be finished with glass or some other transparent or translucent material. What follows applies only to attached greenhouses or freestanding greenhouses with opaque end walls or knee walls.

Any sensible greenhouse builder will want to have maximum insulation where walls are opaque. Part of this insulation may be a polyisocyanurate board or panel. Fire codes require that such material be covered on the interior. Drywall is the generic term most call the trade name Sheetrock, whether it is that brand or some other. Moisture-resistant (MR) Sheetrock is designed for bathrooms; it works very well in an attached greenhouse unless the humidity is much higher than it should be. It can be scored with a utility knife and then broken. Like glasscutting, this takes confidence or perhaps courage. The wallboard can be attached to studs with unique nails; drywall screws applied with a power screwdriver are better. In a house, the wallboard is used working down from the top; the finish flooring and molding cover gaps at the bottom. In a greenhouse, you probably won't have that option.

When you are applying drywall over an insulating board, which involves trying to find the invisible underlying studs with long screws, you'll be mighty glad you put those studs exactly where they were supposed to be. If a pro does the drywall, he'll swear (literally) that they're not.

Putting up the wallboard is one thing we let a pro do in our greenhouse. The job itself is not too difficult for an amateur, but it is difficult for an amateur to have it look perfect when he finishes. After it is "hung," all joints have to be taped. This takes skill if it is not to look lumpy. Some amateurs do the hanging and then hire a professional taper. He'll grumble about the hanging job you did, but don't let it get to you. He would have rolled just as much if a professional, other than he, had done it. Anybody hanging or taping drywall leaves an incredible mess. No matter who does it, you'll have to clean it up.

Chapter - 3
HOW TO BUILD AND DESIGN YOUR GREENHOUSE

CHOOSING YOUR SITE

Determining where your greenhouse is located will be key to your plants' success and the effectiveness of the structure. The more exposure to natural sunlight, the better off you'll be. You can pick a valid location by watching the shadows cast by tall structures like buildings, telephone poles, or trees. Track the sun's movement along the southern horizon by seeing how far the shadows around you extend on your site.

Position your greenhouse as far from the reach of shadows as possible—on the south side if it is feasible. This will allow light to enter the greenhouse even when the sun is lower in the sky during winter months. In the southern hemisphere, you would do the opposite. Pick a flat and level area, or that can be made flat and level by clearing foliage or moving dirt.

LOCAL CODES AND ORDINANCES

Some regions require special regulations or permissions to allow structures to be built on your property. It may depend on size, purpose, or any number of other factors. Before setting out on your greenhouse project, make sure to check with state, county, city, and local groups to make sure you can build the structure you have in mind.

Local codes may limit the design you use—both in the footprint and in scale. You may be limited to a specific size, or you might be required to meet certain engineering standards or construction codes. And in some cases, your greenhouse site may not be zoned for agriculture or commercial production. Most small-scale hobby greenhouses are small enough to dodge this type of regulation. But if your purpose requires more than the codes will allow in your area, you may need to find another site for your greenhouse.

PLUMBING AND ELECTRICAL

Utilities will take some of the work out of maintaining a greenhouse and the plants within. If you can incorporate electricity and plumbing, you can make sure plants are well lit and watered.

Plumbing may take the form of a water supply provided from the main water line, or it may be as simple as a garden hose, hand well, or watering bucket. With any plumbing fed to your greenhouse, you'll want to consider frost protection and the potential for frozen pipes, fittings, and fixtures. If greenhouse vents are not functioning properly or left open during freezing temperatures, you could risk losing internal components to extreme cold.

Internal temperatures can be maintained with lighting, vans, or actuated vents. In order to keep these devices running, you'll need to consider power. Providing electricity on a large scale will require adequate service panels installed by a licensed electrician. For backyard hobby greenhouses, you may be able to meet the needs of a small greenhouse with an extension cord and GFCI surge protectors.

Planning for both plumbing and electrical needs will allow you to provide life-sustaining elements for plants when nature doesn't. However, you'll need to account for your water and electrical needs well in advance to make sure you install appropriately-sized systems.

WATER SOURCES

Before determining the size of your greenhouse, make sure to consider your access to water. The source may be a municipal tower, a well, an aquifer, runoff, or natural water bodies like rivers or lakes. Since water is a critical component to plant growth, you'll want to consider the source and test the water for quality and contamination. Water that looks clean may have significant deposits of toxic chemicals or heavy metals. Chemical additives in municipal water sources may also be harmful to plants. If your water sources are inadequate, you may need to look into alternatives.

Sourcing water can be simple or complex and may be limited in some cases. Depending on your region, you may be able to collect rainwater—where in other areas, it may be illegal. You may have unlimited water rights or limited access due to drought restrictions. Natural water sources like creeks or streams may not be plentiful year-round, and cold weather may hamper your ability to deliver water due to frozen pipes or pumps.

Make sure the location and scale of your greenhouse are within your ability to provide water. If you build a greenhouse that is too big for the amount of water you can supply, your plants will suffer. Be sure to check local restrictions on water use, water storage, and water sources before breaking ground on your greenhouse project.

OFF-GRID OPTIONS

Since greenhouses afford a natural environment for plants of all-weather types, it may make sense to establish a greenhouse off the beaten path. In order to provide additional power and water needs for an off-grid greenhouse, you can look into power generation alternatives like wind or solar. You can also provide water using rainwater collection, cisterns, and gravity-fed systems.

Solar and wind power have the potential to provide for your power needs but will likely limit the options for heat and lighting. In addition, you'll need to account for power storage and less sunlight in the winter months. Still, you may be able to generate enough power for small-scale LED lighting systems if you have enough solar power, batteries, and sunlight to charge your system. To do this, you'll need to size an appropriate system based on average winter sunlight to make sure you can provide for your needs when the sun is at the lowest point of the year. Areas with high winds may be able to supplement solar power and add some wattage to the cause.

Hand watering can be adequate for your greenhouse and would eliminate the need for plumbing. This may take a bit of time and extra care on your part, but it does help to reduce the water consumption and waste caused by spray systems. It may be possible to minimize hand watering efforts by building a system designed around gravity-fed components. Things like water towers, cisterns, and even elevated rain barrels may be adequate forms of pressurized water delivery that won't require grid-tied plumbing. If you can provide pressurized water to your greenhouse, you can introduce drip-feed systems or a simple water source for hand watering

CHOOSING THE CORRECT FOUNDATION

Your foundation is a critical component of the greenhouse. It must serve a few specific functions, including a solid structural base, a stable and washable surface, and a material that can help retain heat.

While greenhouses can incorporate dirt as the foundation, such as simple greenhouse tunnels or cold frames, most hold strong with the help of concrete or solid brick. Concrete and brick foundations allow heat to be absorbed and released slowly long after the sun goes down. It also provides a surface that can support tables, heavy potted plants, structural components and can serve to protect other systems like electrical and plumbing.

Since water is a major component of successful plant growth, you can expect a few spills here and there. Dirt or other loose-fill substrates may contribute to muddy, sloppy surfaces that can become unstable or promote unwanted plant life in your greenhouse. Concrete and brick help to prevent these issues and provide an easy-to-clean surface. If you have a small space or pop-up greenhouse, you can position it on a concrete patio. If no concrete is available, you may be able to substitute with a similar product, like concrete masonry blocks (CMU), asphaltic roofing, or a similar impermeable barrier. Regardless of what you choose, keep in mind that you will want a water-resistant surface that is stable and helps to prevent unwanted plant growth at the ground level.

PREPARING THE SITE FOR A GREENHOUSE

To prepare your site, you'll need a fairly level tract of land or pad, to begin with. This will help limit the workload when developing the greenhouse. The slope and grade will play a key role in water runoff, along with orientation and access.

All plants and vegetation will need to be cleared in advance of the initial work. If you are putting the greenhouse in a vacant lot, you'll need to make sure to provide access for vehicles or equipment and pay close attention to access limitations. You'll also want to consider the damage that could be caused to existing landscaping as a result of tires, heavy equipment, and general traffic. Fences or obstructions may need to be removed.

When the site is cleared and ready for initial dirt work, you can begin with pulling sod and grading the earth to a level starting point. This will require that you call to mark out potential utilities that might be buried below ground. If you intend to frame up an above-ground pad that doesn't require digging, you may still

want to confirm if utilities exist beneath the structure for future reference.

Once these fundamental elements are cleared out, you can start to stake out the ground and run a string level at all corners or the perimeter. This will help to determine the initial level surface so you can cut out or fill it as needed. To find the level point, string a line between one stake and another, and use a line level to adjust the height. Continue this process around the perimeter and make adjustments as you go. You may need to raise or lower your line to complete the task properly. Once your line is level, consider which direction you'll want the water to flow off the floor's surface and off of the roof. Improper water drainage can erode surfaces and cause damage to the foundation. Pooling water inside the greenhouse can create slip hazards. Make sure your water has a path out of the structure and away from the structure.

TOP-NOTCH MATERIALS FOR THE BEST FOUNDATION

Once your base is level, you can choose what kind of materials to incorporate into the foundation. The best way to secure a solid, stable foundation is to start with a layer of aggregate (rock) of a type that tends to lock together when under pressure. River rock is rounded and moves easily compared to fractured rock that locks itself into place.

Once you have a solid base of aggregate, add a fine layer of sand and put it into place. The sand will help to bind larger aggregate into place like mortar on a brick wall. It will also help to prevent weed growth.

At the surface of the rock and sand layer, you may want to include a vapor barrier. This will help prevent moisture from wicking up from the soil below, and it can help avoid destructive plant growth in your foundation. Keep in mind that a greenhouse will provide an ideal location for plants to thrive, and if they find a way to grow, the roots may cause damage to your foundation.

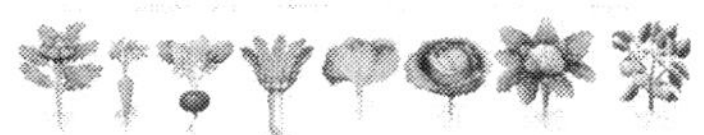

Chapter - 4
CHOOSING THE FRAME AND COVER BEST SUITED FOR YOUR NEEDS AND BUDGET

Greenhouses come in all shapes and sizes. Some pay others to build one for them. Others buy kits and assemble the greenhouse themselves. These options can be quite expensive. The truth is that most people can purchase inexpensive supplies and build their greenhouse from scratch. You can also do so in such a way that at the end of the growing season, it can quickly be taken down if you so desire.

The best reason to have a greenhouse is to extend the growing season. Maybe you live in a part of the country that is prone to late spring freezes. Perhaps you have early winters where you live. Maybe you would like to grow some winter vegetables but may not be able to without the protection that a greenhouse offers. A greenhouse can protect from freezing temperatures and provide sufficient heat for plant growth that would not exist if your vegetables were simply out in the open and subject to the elements/air temperature. A greenhouse can also offer your crops protection from hail and other inclement weather. You may even be able to grow crops that typically could not survive in your area.

The costs may turn some people off because they do not want a greenhouse up all year round for weather or other reasons. In regards to cost, are not so expensive. Those who live in areas that typically receive snow, hail, and other bad weather may not want a greenhouse up year-round. If that is a concern for you, the models I propose can relatively easily be deconstructed.

I am not recommending specific sizes for the frame of your greenhouse. That is up to you. Some people who usually have a large area of vegetables in their backyard may want a large greenhouse; others who only want to grow one or two crops may choose a smaller greenhouse, possibly on their side yard, between their house and fence or another small area.

Some people may design/construct their greenhouse to have tables or other raised platforms to grow their plants on. Such construction may be appropriate when constructing an expensive greenhouse that one never intends to remove, and if the person has back problems and cannot get on the ground to the garden. Such

design is not appropriate for an inexpensive greenhouse that you intend to deconstruct at the end of each growing season. The greenhouses that follow are designed to cover plants that are growing directly in the ground.

Don't use treated lumber because the wood should not be exposed to water and because even if water leaks onto your wooden frame, you do not want chemicals from treated lumber leaching into the ground and onto your crops. If you have back problems, arthritis, or other physical ailments that make lifting and bending a question, a plastic PVC pipe is the better choice for you. If you live in an area that typically gets strong winds in the spring, summer, or fall, wood may be a better choice for your frame.

Let us begin by discussing a PVC frame. You can go to your local home improvement store and buy this type in ten-foot lengths. The most convenient shape to fashion this into a greenhouse is an oval or egg-shaped greenhouse. If you want a somewhat broad and tall greenhouse, you could use two ten-piece PVC pipes, one on each side, and connect them at the greenhouse roof. How many of these you need to be determined by how long you want your greenhouse to go. I also recommend you have one piece of PVC pipe running lengthwise along the roof to fasten the side pieces. This increases the structural integrity of the greenhouse. You can join the connections with PVC connectors, zip ties, or even duct tape in a pinch. Then on one side of the greenhouse, fashion a door frame out of PVC pipe and a door with lengths of PVC running width wise and height wise. The door can be fastened to the frame using zip ties.

The other option is to make a greenhouse frame entirely out of wood. Most people do not shape greenhouse-like oval. Instead, they build the sides and roof like A-frame shape with the sides directly straight up perpendicular to the ground and the two sides of the top coming together like the shape of the letter A, much like the shape of a roof on most residential house. I should note here that sometimes people who construct their greenhouse entirely out of PVC pipe also make it in the A-frame fashion instead of an oval shape, but the oval shape is more prevalent when using an entire PVC pipe frame.

One potential disadvantage of using wood to construct your greenhouse frame is the potential for sharp edges to damage the greenhouse plastic used for the windows. Accordingly, if you use wood, try to make sure the pieces fit together well, and you may need to take a power sander to sand off any sharp edges.

If using wood, construct a door out of wood, and build a wooden frame around the door. Attach the entrance to the frame with metal hinges and screws. You could install an inexpensive doorknob like you would use on an interior door of a house to keep your wooden door closed.

It would help if you decided how far apart to space your side supports, which create your greenhouse walls. I recommend every two and a half to three feet. If you use wood, you might be tempted to space them further apart because you think wood is more robust than PVC, so you do not need as many supports. I would resist this temptation because the purpose of the PVC or wood is to hold the frame together and give adequate support to the plastic sheeting used as windows.

When constructing your greenhouse frame out of wood, you could use screws or nails to fasten wood pieces together. When deconstructing the greenhouse, if you used screws to attach the wood, you should remove the screws with a screw gun relatively quickly. If you intend to use nails, I recommend using nails designed for laying form boards for concrete. These nails have two heads, one that is pounded down to the base of the wood, and the other is left exposed to make removing the nail much more manageable once the concrete is set and the form boards are then removed.

Once your frame is complete, you are ready to wrap the frame in plastic greenhouse sheeting. Take care when attaching the sheeting so that you do not cut or tear it. This process is easier/faster if you have one person on each side of the greenhouse. If you have a third person standing around doing nothing, you could even have them stand in the middle of the greenhouse. The greenhouse might be tall enough that that person in the middle might not be able to reach the sheeting with their hands. They could use a soft mop to reach up and help push the sheeting down the length of the greenhouse as the two people on both sides pull the sheeting. Start at one end of the greenhouse, pull the plastic sheeting up and over and then pull it down the greenhouse.

It is then time to fasten your plastic sheeting to the bottom of the frame. It should be fastened somewhat tight, but not so tight that it cannot move slightly, which it will need to do when the temperature changes. Extend it over your greenhouse and slightly past the bottom of the greenhouse. You could use screws to fasten the sheeting to the bottom of the greenhouse frame. You could also use staples. There are also specific types of tape just for this purpose, such as polypropylene batten tape.

Construct your greenhouse early in the spring, so you are ready to plant early on. Remember that you can plant your crops earlier than usual with a greenhouse because of the warmth it will create. If living in a region with below-freezing temperatures, you will not plant so long as the ground is still frozen. Setting up your greenhouse may help the environment below your greenhouse thaw quicker than it otherwise would. Also, if you intend to set up a table or other platform and put plants on top of it, waiting for the ground to thaw is not such a concern.

At the end of the growing season, you are now in a position to deconstruct your greenhouse easily. On the other hand, some people build this type of greenhouse but then decide for various reasons to leave the greenhouse up. If you do this, I still recommend you remove the plastic greenhouse sheeting.

How long will your plastic sheeting last? If it is quality sheeting, and it has not been damaged during the growing season, there is no reason you could not get three years or more of use out of it. For this to happen, you should carefully remove it at the end of each growing season. Carefully remove the screws, staples, wires, or whatever you used to fasten the sheeting, and then gingerly roll it up. Before reinstalling the sheeting before the growing season, wash the sheeting with soap and warm water to remove dirt, dead bugs, and the like so that it will be clear enough to let sufficient light through.

Your total costs in constructing your greenhouse will be determined based on how big/long you decide to make your greenhouse. I would expect a typical one you might construct in your urban/suburban backyard; you can do so for less than $200. This money will be quickly offset when you start picking produce in your backyard instead of buying it at the supermarket.

Some people do something else with a small portable greenhouse. They use it only as a starter of sorts. Let us say, for example, they want to grow. Maybe they normally plant them at the beginning of June, but they would like to plant them early. They plant them on May 1st and immediately cover them with a small PVC greenhouse like the one mentioned here. Then around June 1st or June 15th, when the weather is much warmer and the sun is blazing hot, they remove the greenhouse. They only needed the greenhouse to extend the growing season at the beginning of the season.

Greenhouses do not have to be expensive or permanent. For a small investment, most people can fairly easily construct a portable greenhouse that will extend their growing season, and that can easily be removed at the end of the growing season if you so choose.

Chapter - 5
USEFUL POINTERS TO HELP YOU CHOOSE THE RIGHT LOCATION

You can only have one potential place to install a greenhouse in your backyard. But if you have the choice, then it is worth offering the best possible role you can. You can maximize the efficiency of your greenhouse system with diligent site selection that lets you offset the area it takes up in your garden, the time and energy expended on creating it, as well as the initial outlay.

You'll need a spot that has the most solar radiation exposure.

For photosynthesis, your plants need at least six hours of exposure to sunlight. Plants require the cycle to grow healthily and bear fruits or flowers. The best way of sitting depends largely on the season you want the plants to grow.

Face the East-West Pass. Lining up the east to the west ridge of the structure maximizes light interception, particularly during November through January. Following cold nights the route will help crops heat up faster.

Road faces south. This seating position is only preferable if you intend to expand your crops during the season. The path would be transmitted on either side of the system, producing an equivalent volume of light and helping minimize too much heat output.

Please note: If necessary, avoid the north side of your home because the plants are constrained by the amount of sunshine in this field, unless you are willing to allow extra light and heat sources. Bear in mind, too, those shady areas will restrict the amount of sunshine your greenhouse can get. The shadow lines range from summer to winter. It is advised that a greenhouse should be at a maximum equal to at least twice the height of any potential source of shade.

A new study also shows that the latitude of a position on your system will be a criterion for your desired orientation. For eg, a North-South orientation is optimal to provide good light and better ventilation for southern latitudes where there is a colder climate. Further, the wind's power and speed can also be taken into account. Outdoor planting on windy fields is very difficult.

Opt for a place where you'll be windproof like trees, but but make sure it doesn't create too much shadowing. Make sure the site has good access to water, power, and other required services. For practical planting, you'll need a place near a water supply, power, and electricity. In planting, the watering system is important, particularly if a natural supply of water such as rain or groundwater is limited. It is safe to research the land profile before setting out one. Best still, pick a place where you can easily layout your irrigation water. It also works the same for the energy required in lawnmowers, hedge trimmers, along with outside lighting, pond pumps, and greenhouse heaters supplying fuel. Fire and electrocution must be stopped with caution.

A secure elevated land is required to avoid the accumulation of excess water. Although irrigation is important to plant growth, they may also suffer or die from overwatering, which is caused mostly by rain flooding or excess water falling off the roof. It is better to build the system on an elevated field, and runoff flows away from the greenhouse seamlessly.

Further note: You can theoretically orient a greenhouse on a slope but stop doing so. You would need a higher elevated soil but placing it in a sloping base would frost the pocket where coldness lingers, particularly for winter farming.

Find a place where plants can grow good soil or the ability to do so. If you're not entirely sure of the soil type, you'll need to employ an expert to examine the soil's mineral, structure, and composition. Digging into the organic matter will strengthen weak soil. Yet when you can find an environment with outstanding planting soil and natural drainage, you would require no planning to grow it, minimizing weed seed bank, and introducing organic matter.

Additional note: Seek to avoid rocky or stony terrain because it may be a hiccup in the building process.

Finally, the extension capacity of a site is good too. Expansion requirements are often uncertain. You will require a bigger area for your crops in the future, or you may need an improvement in your plant count. Construction of a greenhouse in a wide area is also suitable to prepare for the prospect of extension.

Chapter - 6

CHOOSE THE BEST TYPE OF GLASS, FLOORING, CONSTRUCTION MATERIAL, AND FOUNDATION TO ENSURE OUR GREENHOUSE HAS A LONG LIFE AND CAN WITHSTAND VARIOUS FACTOR

TEMPERED GLASS

These are strong and impact resistant. This means that they will withstand any expansions or contractions during the seasonal temperature changes. The 3mm single pane thickness is ideal for the greenhouse.

However, the 4mm thickness is much stronger and will provide additional insulation. You must protect the hedges during insulation, as the glass may shatter if hit hard. Tempered glass is much more expensive compared to polycarbonate panels.

Tempered glass is more durable even if it's expensive, and it is more resistant to scratches and very clear, and provides no diffusion.

FIBERGLASS

This is translucent and provides a light that is well-diffused. Fiberglass retains heat better than normal glass. The greenhouses made from fiberglass are normally corrugated to provide adequate rigidity because the outer coat will become sunbaked within 6-10 years. The surface will become etched and yellow.

ALUMINUM

This will provide a very strong frame that does not rust, and it's lightweight. It has a very long lifespan, and it's the most widely used frame for greenhouses. Aluminum has extruding channels, which are perfect for inserting the covering panels.

STEEL

Steel that is galvanized is a very strong and long-lasting plus; it's reasonably priced. Because of its strength, you require just a little for the framing, which adds the amount of light passing on to the plants.

Steel is also very heavy and ensures the greenhouse remains solid no matter the weather conditions or temperature levels. However, the transportation and assembling of the greenhouse can be difficult since the steel is heavy.

PLASTIC RESIN

These are very attractive and are very popular. This is because, compared to aluminum, they are less expensive, and they also do not conduct any heat away from the greenhouse-like steel does.

POLYCARBONATE

It is UV-treated, lightweight and durable. It is high quality and modern material used for greenhouses. The polycarbonate is available in different thickness levels and provides the clarity of glass, but it's not scratching resistant, or as strong as tempered glass.

The single-walled one does not retain any heat and provides no light diffusion. It, however, has a longer lifespan of more than 15 years, depending on the region.

TWIN-WALLED POLYCARBONATE

This is very popular because it has internal spaces providing strength and excellent insulation. The best point to note about the twin-walled polycarbonate is that it diffuses light.

Triple-Walled Polycarbonate

This is similar to twin-walled polycarbonate, but it has extra strength and heat retention abilities. In cold climates, the triple-walled polycarbonate is extremely useful for all-year-round indoor gardening because it will withstand snow loads and will freeze without cracking or distorting.

FOUNDATION

When you are building a greenhouse, the first step is to build a foundation. This needs to be done properly for you to have a solid greenhouse that will stand the test time.

Whatever you decide to make your foundation out of, it needs to be both level and square. You can buy pre-made greenhouse bases, and these are worth considering, but just be aware that these still need a flat and level surface to be installed on and will still need a foundation beneath them.

When building your greenhouse base, you can either make it out of poured concrete, or you can use sand and paving stones. Both are suitable and do the job well, though the latter has the advantage of being moveable in the future if necessary.

Ensure that not only are the edges of your base square but also that the diagonal measurements between the corners are also identical.

Under the base, you will need a good foundation to support the weight of the greenhouse which is secured to, preventing damage in windy weather.

If you live in an area where the ground freezes, your greenhouse foundation needs to be below the frost line.

This is to prevent damage structure as the ground freezes and melts. Your local Building Permit Agency will be able to tell you where the frost line is in your area. In warmer areas, this is only going to be a couple of inches at most, but in the colder, northern areas it can be as much as a few feet.

One good way of insulating your foundation and protecting it is to use 1" foam insulation. Put this down to your frost line to reduce heat loss through the soil, which has the benefit of reducing your heating costs.

The foundation is essential because this is what you are securing your greenhouse to. It will prevent weather damage and warping in hot or cold weather. If you do not secure your greenhouse properly, then don't expect it to last the growing season. If the greenhouse starts to warp, then you can find your panes shatter or crack and become very hard to re-fit. You can also find doors and windows become stiff and very difficult to use too.

If you have bought a new greenhouse, then any warranty will not cover damage due to not having a proper greenhouse base.

Your greenhouse is built on this foundation and base, which will ensure it is easier to erect and that it will last.

There are some different choices for the foundation; they are:

COMPACTED SOIL

If you compact the soil large enough, you can build the greenhouse directly on the ground, especially if you live in an area where ground freezing is not too severe.

A lot of greenhouses will come with an optional metal plinth that has spikes in each corner. These can be cemented into the ground to prevent the base from moving.

You will still need to level the ground, though, so dig out your spirit level. It is best to use a roller or other mechanical device to compact the soil to ensure it is stable. Do not build your base out of gravel or hardcore because these are just not stable enough.

The advantage of using the soil as your foundation is that it is very cost-effective. You can also use the existing ground for growing your plants in plus drainage is a lot better.

The downside of soil is that it will allow pests into your greenhouse. You will find this particularly bad in winter as pests flock to your greenhouse for warmth.

PERIMETER BASES

This is a slightly cheaper option where you use either bricks, breeze blocks, or thin paving or edging slabs to create a foundation directly under the greenhouse frame. You can use concrete if you prefer.

The foundation is built along where the frame will run, leaving the soil in the middle of the greenhouse untouched.

While you can build the foundation directly on the soil, most people will cut out a trench and place the foundation in the trench. The advantage of this latter approach is that it is easier to level.

It is very easy to prepare and can be very decorative. However, you have to be very accurate with your measurements because there isn't a lot of room for error.

SLABS OR PAVING

This is a very popular way to build your greenhouse foundation because it keeps out the weeds and pests while giving you a good, clean growing environment.

This method involves building a base the size of your greenhouse out of paving slabs and then fixing your greenhouse to it. This type of base will last for many years and is very low maintenance.

You can screw your greenhouse to the base to provide stability in windy conditions, preventing any damage. It also provides good drainage when compared to an all-concrete base.

In the winter months, a soil floor can get damp and encourage mold to grow. A paved floor helps to keep the greenhouse both warmer and drier in the cooler months.

However, this is more expensive to build and requires more work. You will also not be able to grow directly in the soil and have to use containers and grow bags, which most people consider necessary in a greenhouse.

CONCRETE BASE

This is where you mark out where your greenhouse will be and dig down a few inches before pouring concrete in to form the base.

GREENHOUSE FLOOR

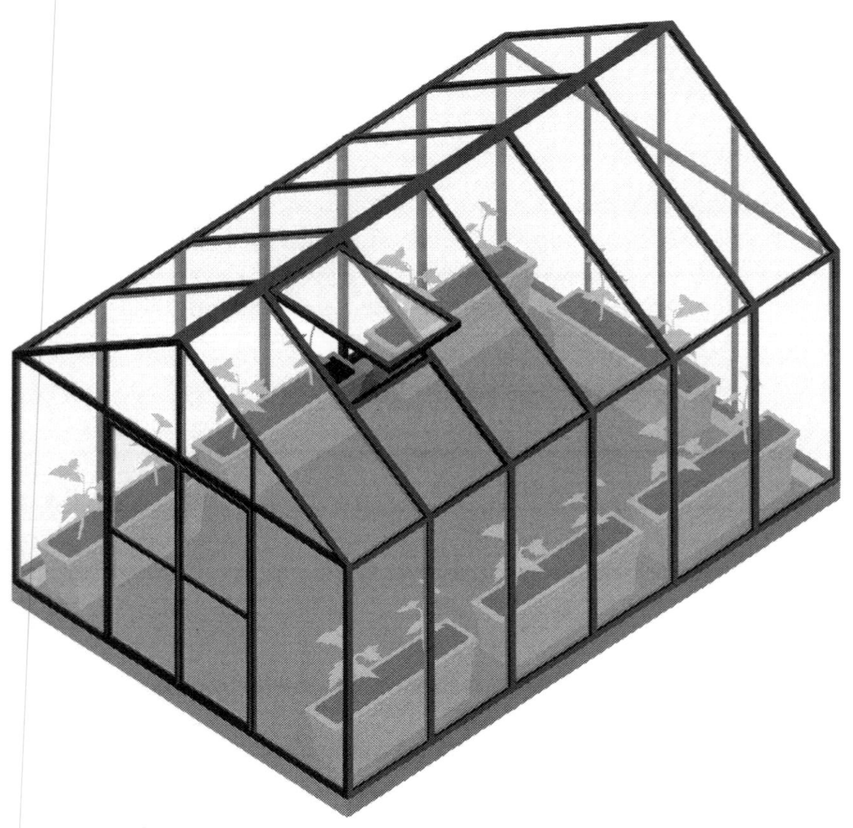

Drainage is very important in a greenhouse as if the environment is too damp then it will encourage mold, and your plants will rot.

Although you can use compacted soil, it comes with a whole host of potential problems that will make growing in a greenhouse more difficult, increasing your workload over the year. In most cases, the disadvantages of compacted soil far outweigh the advantages.

Before you lay any floor though, the first thing to do is put down a good quality weed membrane. Don't

skimp here and buy the cheap fabric, as that will let the weeds through. Spend the extra money to buy an outstanding quality woven plastic membrane, and this will prevent weeds from getting into your greenhouse.

Don't be tempted to use a normal plastic liner because these are not water permeable. Water will pool on top of the plastic liner and flood your greenhouse. Although you can make holes in the plastic liner to let water through, doing so will let the weeds come up into the greenhouse.

If you are laying paving slabs, you need to put sand underneath them, which will help drainage. With mortared slabs or a concrete floor, you will need to install some drainage holes to allow water to drain away. Just ensure that your drainage holes do not allow weeds to get in.

Start your paving slab floor by laying an excellent quality membrane underneath it. Cover this with about 2" of finely crushed rock. Then build a frame of treated wood that follows the edge of your greenhouse and marks out any walkways. Then spread sand to about 1" deep, pressing it down firmly. Lay your pavers, leaving about ½" between each one. Then fill the gaps with sand, using a brush to clear sand off the slabs.

A concrete floor is laid with a little bit more consideration. You have to work out how you are going to drain the floor before you start to lay it. In most cases, the floor will have plastic tubes going down into the soil, which excess water drains into. Under each tube will be a drain sump, i.e. a large amount of gravel to ensure water soaks away quickly and doesn't back up the tube to flood the greenhouse.

Alternatively, you can make the floor slightly slanted, so water drains off to one side, and there you place your drain sump.

The advantage of a concrete floor is that it is easy to clean and will retain heat though it is more time-consuming and costly to install.

Before pouring your concrete floor, you will dig down a couple of inches. You need to fill the base with about 2" of gravel and tamp it down to ensure it is well packed.

On top of this, the concrete is poured between an inch or two deep, depending on your needs. Once the base has dried, build a 2x4" wood sill on which you anchor your greenhouse.

Countersink the nuts into the wood sill and the greenhouse attached to this. Set the bolts within a foot of each corner with additional bolts every 3 to 4 feet.

This is a very important part of constructing a greenhouse and must be done properly to avoid problems and extra expense in the future. Do this well, and it will give you years of service!

WOOD VS. ALUMINUM FRAMES

Wooden frames look great on a greenhouse, but they are more expensive and will require regular maintenance. You will need to treat the wood annually to prevent it from decay and maintain its beauty. Eventually, though the wood will need replacing, it can be difficult and time-consuming to replace single wood pieces.

Wooden-framed greenhouses look great and when looked after will last for many years. Because of their weight and natural strength, they are less susceptible to wind damage. So if you live in an area with high winds, then it may be worth investing in a wooden frame to prevent damage to your greenhouse.

All you need to do is bolt it all together, though you will need help due to the weight of the wood and the size of the panels.

Aluminum frames are much cheaper to buy and will usually come flat packed, so you have to assemble them yourself. They will also usually fit in your car so you can take them home then and there rather than wait for delivery.

This does mean you can do a lot of it by yourself as it is much lighter than wood, but it is also more likely to twist. With an aluminum greenhouse, you need to ensure that the greenhouse is square and level, which can take time.

Although much more affordable than wood, aluminum is a lot lighter. This means you need to take extra care to secure it to the ground to prevent wind damage. High winds will tear an aluminum greenhouse to pieces, twisting the frame and shattering the glass. When properly secured though, it can survive all but the most severe storms.

Powder coating is a chemical process that coats the aluminum frame with colored powder. This is baked on. The range of colors available is good though you will need to get your greenhouse from a supplier that offers this service. You can expect to pay a high price for this paint.

Which you choose is up to you, but most of us will go for aluminum frames purely from an affordability point of view.

Chapter - 7
WHAT TO LOOK FOR WHEN BUYING A NEW OR USED GREENHOUSE

Buying a new greenhouse is just too expensive for many. They aren't cheap, and the cost means many people do not buy one.

A good option is to buy a used greenhouse either through eBay, Freecycle, Gumtree, or local ads. Often these are a fraction of the price of a new greenhouse, and you can even find greenhouses for free! Some people, when they move into a new home, find a greenhouse they don't want and will offer it for free to someone who is willing to come and take it away.

When buying a used greenhouse, you will be expected, in many cases, to disassemble the greenhouse yourself. Take lots of pictures of the greenhouse before you take it apart, as it will help you to put it back together again. Make notes on any non-standard panes and where they belong. Plenty of pictures from all angles is the easiest way to do this.

Taking a greenhouse down and reassembling it will be a two-person job, so you need to find yourself a helper to make the job easier.

You will need some tools to take down the greenhouse, including a wide selection of spanners, both open and closed-ended. You will also need a variety of screwdrivers, both flat and cross-head, and also large ones. A ratchet spanner will help you a lot and make things easier. A good pair of pliers can also help with the more stubborn bolts.

I would also recommend a can of WD-40 to help ease rusted bolts as well as a junior hacksaw for those exceptionally stubborn bolts.

You should wear gloves, particularly while moving the glass; otherwise, you will end up with plenty of cuts on your hands.

Ideally, you will want to disassemble the greenhouse on a dry day because doing it in the rain is unpleasant (trust me on this) and much harder as everything becomes slippery.

It is worthwhile labeling parts as you take them apart as it will help you a lot when putting it back together. If you can get a van, then you don't have to take the greenhouse down completely. You can just break it into the front, rear, and side panels and the two halves of the roof and fit them in the van. It will save you a lot of work if you can do it this way!

Most used greenhouses will be on the smaller side, usually 8x6' or thereabouts. If you want a larger greenhouse, then just get two smaller greenhouses and join them together!

As with any greenhouse, the first thing you need to do is build a base following instructions. Just make sure that the base is square (measure the diagonals) and level (use a spirit level that is at least 3 feet long).

Before you dive headlong into assembling your greenhouse, you need to sort out all the bits and pieces. Ensure you have enough nuts and bolts and that those you have are usable. Sometimes they can be rusted or the thread stripped, so you will want to have enough to hand. The last thing you want to do is to go halfway when you find that important parts are missing. Buy from most home improvement stores or online.

Also, make sure you have plenty of glass clips as these often go missing or get broken when taking a greenhouse to pieces.

Make sure all the glass pieces are present and none are broken. You cannot assemble your greenhouse without all the panes, as that will make it extremely susceptible to wind damage.

Check the weather forecast before you start building your greenhouse, as doing it in the rain is no fun and doing it in high winds is positively dangerous!

Sort the struts out, group them together into each of the sides and the roof. This allows you to check you have all the pieces and then assemble each side before you put it all together.

After the frame is assembled, you need to start placing the glass in place. This is best done from the top down because you can get around the greenhouse better without glass in the frame beneath you. This is when you realize that your glazing clips are broken, twisted, or even missing, so buy a bag or two before you start! Remember that glass doesn't bend, so you need to be careful putting it in. An 8x6' greenhouse can end up using up to 200 of these clips!

It is also worthwhile buying some extra rubber seals that the glass fits into. Invariably when taking a greenhouse to pieces, these will break or get lost.

Buy all the spare parts you need before you start reassembling the greenhouse. It will make your life much easier.

Just remember to be careful when reassembling your greenhouse. The glass can and will break, so transport

it with care. It isn't a race, so just take your time and make sure you have someone to help you!

Chapter - 8
WHY AIRFLOW AND COOLING ARE SO VITAL AND HOW TO PREVENT HUMIDITY DAMAGING YOUR PLANTS

Do you recall how growing up, you learned all about planting a seed? You discovered the requirements to make the seed grow, including sun and water. You may have even learned about the importance of temperature for a growing plant. The growing space temperature is critical, and if it is too hot or too cold, you can kill your plants.

The greatest advantage of greenhouses is that you can regulate the temperature inside them if you know-how.

If you are successful at regulating the temperature, your plants will not be vulnerable to extreme weather conditions that will kill them. However, when controlling the temperature, you must consider both the amount of heat needed when it's cold and cool off the greenhouse when it's too hot.

At the height of summer, a greenhouse can be excessively stuffy and steamy if it lacks proper cooling systems. The most problematic aspect of this is the damaging impact of heat on the plants. Extremely hot temperatures cause heat stress in plants, which will impact their health and damage their growth. The ideal is a steady, moderate temperature. This can be done by regulating the cooling and ventilation systems in the greenhouse.

To function most effectively as an ideal growing environment, greenhouses also need the right combination of shade, humidity, and ventilation. This reinforces the importance of maximizing the opportunities for controlling your greenhouse environment using cooling systems.

CONSIDER THE SIZE OF THE GREENHOUSE

Before making a final decision about your cooling system, you must first consider your greenhouse size since this affects the device you need. For example, getting a high horsepower mechanical cooling system for a tiny greenhouse might be overwhelming for the available space. Always ascertain the right fit for any greenhouse components based on your gardening space's size and specific needs.

VENTILATING GREENHOUSES

Another great way of cooling your greenhouse is through ventilation. Ventilation provides a good flow of air through vents at the rooftop or the sides. This air movement reduces heat and humidity in the growing space. There are different ways to achieve adequate ventilation, and we will discuss some of them below.

To successfully ventilate your space, the size of the floor area, roof, and all sides must be considered so air can flow evenly. You must get a sufficient volume of air moving through space, not just within the room. For example, one roof vent may only assist in cooling a small area. You can get additional ventilation using side vents and by opening the entrance.

Unless you are expecting frost or a very chilly night, such as the ones common at the beginning and end of the growing season, keep the vents open all the time, including on warm nights. To prevent wildlife and pests, install a screen or net over the door. Some greenhouses come with automatic vent openers already installed.

SHADING

Shading is another crucial technique for fighting off heat in the greenhouse, and if you use it wisely, you will achieve the perfect environment in your growing space. Your plants will grow to their full potential when the greenhouse temperature and the sun's intensity are moderated by shading. Shading paints are a cost-effective way of filtering excessive sunlight and preventing sunburn on your plants.

You can also add layers of paint to the exterior of your building as summer progresses and gets hotter. Shade paint is suitable for most greenhouses. You can also shade your greenhouse using blinds installed either on the interior or exterior of the structure. External blinds filter sunlight even before it passes through the glass, and the heat gets trapped inside the greenhouse. The most affordable blinds are sometimes made from mesh or netting.

When the weather is more relaxed and the sun is not as intense, you can remove the shading material. However, you must be mindful when you take off the blinds because the weather can suddenly change.

DAMPING

During extreme hot weather conditions, you can keep the plants fresher through the damping technique. Damping is when you wet the greenhouse surfaces such as pathways, hard surfaces, and walls. This raises the humidity inside the greenhouse because as water evaporates, the air's moisture levels increase, helping the plants cope with the heat. One of the other benefits of growing the humidity in the greenhouse is that many pests cannot thrive in such an environment. High humidity will increase the occurrence of diseases such as powdery mildew.

You may wonder, "How often can I damp my greenhouse?" You can do it daily when the weather is scorching, but it is best done first thing in the morning. This creates an optimal level of humidity throughout the day.

HOW TO AVOID WATER STRESS IN PLANTS

Plants with controlled amounts of water grow better than plants that receive water inconsistently. Thus, being dedicated to your watering routine is crucial to the success of your garden.

When plants are scorching, they transpire. Transpiration is an efficient way to keep themselves fresh; through moisture loss in the leaf pore (the stomata). This heat loss cools the leaf down on the surface just like when we sweat: imagine if you couldn't sweat?

When moisture is lost, it must be replenished by watering. If the leaf transpires and then has no water source, it cannot sweat and will when it overheats. To avoid stress in your plants, you need to pay close attention to observing heat and water stress signs. If the plant's wilt, becomes scorched, or dry out, it means there is a water problem.

When you become diligent and intentional about keeping your plants adequately moist in a greenhouse, you will prevent stress that could decrease plant health.

EVAPORATIVE COOLING

Evaporative cooling has to do with the evaporation of water from the greenhouse. This is typically done either through recirculating evaporative pad cooling machines or high-pressure fog systems. With evaporative pads, you use mechanical fans that pull the air through a wet pad. As the ambient air passes through the pad, the moisture cools the air.

Evaporative air coolers are self-contained units with evaporative pads and a blower. These units are mostly used in smaller greenhouses and mounted outside the structure. They blow moist air into the greenhouse through an opening on the sidewall.

Another option for evaporative cooling is high-pressure fogging, which is useful for both natural and mechanically ventilated greenhouses.

High-pressure fog is an effective way of cooling and controlling the greenhouse environment as it uses less water than the pad and blower system. This system doesn't only cool the air; it also contains any vapor pressure deficit in the greenhouse.

MECHANICAL VENTILATION

Mechanical ventilation is one of the most sought-after kinds of ventilation for greenhouses because it is easily controlled. With this option, you can get natural ventilation benefits and still maintain the airflow through mechanical means if necessary.

Mechanical ventilation improves airflow by extracting warm air out of the greenhouse and allowing cold air in. To use mechanical ventilation, you need first to consider the greenhouse size, as this will dictate how many fans you will need to cool the volume of air inside.

Fans are selected based on the cubic feet per minute they will move air, the fans' static pressure, horsepower rating, and size. After setting up the fans, you can control their cooling rates using a thermostat or an environmental control system. This degree of control and involvement is essential with mechanical ventilation because you don't want to leave the fan on without checking that the greenhouse temperature is correct.

NATURAL VENTILATION

This type of ventilation allows for natural airflow and exchange within and outside the greenhouse space. For this kind of cooling system, the greenhouse is designed to have multiple vents, making it easier for air to enter and exit the greenhouse.

Properly placed vents maximize the natural airflow through the structure, allowing excess heat to exit, enhancing the moisture level, and optimizing the exchange of oxygen and carbon dioxide.

One reason growers struggle with natural ventilation is if they didn't consider it before building their greenhouses. Once a structure is created, it is harder to add ventilation. When designing your conservatory, consider your cooling and ventilation needs.

Natural ventilation is an excellent supplement to other cooling systems you may be considering. Natural ventilation is also a great backup if any of your mechanical cooling systems suddenly fail.

COOLING MAINTENANCE

Lastly, you've got to ensure that your cooling equipment is properly managed and maintained for long-term use. Regardless of the cost of cooling equipment, you should take good care of everything to ensure optimal operation and prevent malfunctions. You cannot afford a broken ventilator or cooling system when the weather is scorching. Plants are so vulnerable to heat that only one day of overheating can cause a full crop failure.

All cooling equipment should be cleaned regularly, monitored, and protected from sudden electrical surges. Keep the units free from algae and keep areas where cooling systems are installed free from weeds.

For evaporative cooling, please make sure the doors to your structure are closed when the fan is operational so the air properly circulates. If you leave the door open, the fan will be overworked without yielding the right results. Randomly check the cooling systems for changes in performance levels and fix any issues immediately.

Cooling down your greenhouse is a compulsory aspect of effective greenhouse management because regulating the temperatures and protecting your plants from heat and water stress is crucial for a successful growing experience.

There are many options to choose from when considering the purchase and installation of a greenhouse cooling system. When you are ready to buy your cooling equipment, consider your specific needs and budget.

Chapter - 9

THE BEST WAY TO HEAT YOUR GREENHOUSE AND THE DIFFERENCES BETWEEN THE DIFFERENT HEATING SYSTEMS

Now that you understand the importance of a cooling system, let's talk about heating systems, which can also be an essential part of the greenhouse operation. Just as we try to cool the greenhouse when it is hot, we should also ensure that it is warm enough at the beginning and end of the growing seasons and in winter if needed.

Growers must be intentional about maintaining the right temperature in their greenhouses so the plants can grow bountifully. However, heating a greenhouse in the winter can be challenging, hence using mechanical heating systems that enable a balanced temperature to be maintained.

In times past, most growers didn't concern themselves with heat system efficiency or emissions. They only ensured the heat was available without considering its impact on the environment. As interest in climate change increases, growers have started to pay attention to their heating methods' potential impact. Many greenhouses use fossil fuels such as natural gas, coal, or fuel oil for heat. More environmentally friendly options are powered by electricity.

Heating systems have to be affordable, safe for long-term use, and efficient. All heat sources should be close enough to the plants to support their growing needs while maintaining enough distance to be safe.

Let's consider two major categories of heating systems:

- Central heating
- Heating system replacements

Both categories of products can effectively heat greenhouses, and there are various products within each category. Always consider your needs and budget and then pick what will work best for you.

THE FIRST CATEGORY: THE CENTRAL HEATING SYSTEM

With a central heating system, the heat is transferred from a hot water pipe to an object. This is often referred to as "radiant heat." This type of heating system utilizes boilers to heat water or produce steam, and the boilers can burn fuel like natural gas, coal, or fuel oil.

These hot water systems are very efficient for greenhouses, and one of the beneficial by-products of the boiler is CO2. This gas remains in the greenhouse to help the plants achieve photosynthesis. This technique is not usually practical for a small-scale greenhouse because it requires the installation of expensive hardware.

In this system, the warm water or steam has to be transported through pipes around the greenhouse. This process's efficiency is higher than forced air, which we will discuss soon. The pipes used for this technique can be placed around the greenhouse if it is a stand-alone structure.

The greenhouse floor can also be heated with hot water pipes that are placed on the ground under a layer of concrete, sand, soil, or gravel. The heating pipes loop around throughout the entire greenhouse floor surface.

INFRARED RADIANT HEATER

With the infrared radiant heater, heat moves from its source to an object in the greenhouse. The heat is transferred from the pipe to the plants. With this technique, air doesn't move the heat, and air temperature will not increase, yet the plant will be warm.

This technique requires an infrared pipe or two pipes that run through the length of the greenhouse. The method also consists of a single burner or several burners depending on the greenhouse and the pipe's size. With this method, finned pipes are better than bare pipes because they work best with a larger surface area, thus radiating heat evenly.

The infrared heating system delivers more heat when placed so that it faces the plants and can cover the greenhouse's entire scope. This method's fuel source can either be natural gas or propane, and these low-intensity infrared heaters are safer to use in greenhouses than high-intensity alternatives.

FORCED AIR HEATERS

The forced air heater can be either vented or unvented. With a vented forced air heater, the combustion heat is transferred to the air through a heat exchanger. The exhaust gases from the combustion must be delivered outside the greenhouse using a flue pipe. Then the oxygen for the combustion is obtained from the environment outside the greenhouse.

For the second option, the unvented forced air heater, the oxygen is obtained from the inside of the structure. The shortcoming of this system is that the gases from combustion remain inside the greenhouse, as all the heat produced by the heater is maximized to heat the air.

The fuel sources used for forced air heaters are either gas, kerosene, or fuel oil, and the by-products of the combustion include: carbon dioxide, vapor, carbon monoxide, and ethylene. Plants can maximize the use of carbon dioxide, but the other gases will need to be vented. These heaters can be mounted overhead in the greenhouse or placed on the floor, thus enabling heating from the top or the bottom.

Forced-air heating units can be placed in different parts of the greenhouse, and all units used simultaneously. This heating system also requires fans to move the air from the heater to the other greenhouse side. A great way of achieving this airflow is by using polyethylene tubes.

The polyethylene tube will be parallel to the length of the greenhouse and its plant rows. The tubes come with ventilation holes so that it distributes heat evenly to the plants. This heat distribution method is one of the best as it not only releases heat inside the greenhouse; it also ensures that the plants get warmth directly.

Most small greenhouse owners can attest to this method's viability because smaller greenhouses are more heavily impacted by extreme cold. With one heater and an overhead polyethylene pipe, you can heat a greenhouse.

Moreover, smaller diameter polyethylene tubes can be on the benches' side, under the plant rows, and between them. If you want to move air through the whole greenhouse, you might install a horizontal airflow fan. These fans enable proper air circulation such that there is no stagnant air or high humidity air pockets. This protects the plants from developing certain diseases caused by excessive heat and stagnant air in the greenhouse.

This heater can be set to automatically turn on and off based on the temperature on the thermostat. Compared to a central heating system, it takes less time to heat the air, which means it gradually provides warmth to the greenhouse instead of the instant hot air, which could overwhelm the plant.

A most striking feature about the forced air heaters is their versatility. These heaters are so versatile that they can be used with any greenhouse regardless of the size. The option to use multiple units in larger greenhouses also makes it one of the most sought-after heating systems.

THE SECOND CATEGORY: THE HEATING SYSTEM REPLACEMENT

The heating system replacement refers to replacing a furnace or boiler when they are no longer safe (when it gets to less than 70% efficiency). The heating system should also be replaced when emissions rise above 10% of the recommended EPA standard.

Professional installers should monitor a new heating replacement system's design and installation to ensure proper and safe operation.

CONDENSING BOILERS AND HEATERS

Water vapor results from the combustion of gas or oil, and this water vapor, with other products, goes up and is exhausted into the atmosphere. With the condensing boiler, extra heat is incorporated into the gas exhaust system, making the water vapor condense back to liquid.

The condensing boilers are most effective when the return water is cool. Under the right conditions, condensing boilers can guarantee 95% efficiency for your greenhouse. However, you should know that condensing boilers and heaters are more expensive than regular boilers. They are a good option because they reliably offer great results.

COMBUSTION TECHNOLOGY

This technique requires using a conventional burner where fuel is continuously injected under pressure. The method uses a specific fuel-air ratio, and it requires an ignition spark to start the burning process. The advantage of combustion technology is that you get a higher efficiency heating system because of the airflow process's uniformity.

HEAT STORAGE BUFFER TANK

The heat storage buffer tank is an old heating system that has been used since the 1970s as part of a solar system. This method is being used in greenhouses and other spaces where industrial plants are grown. This heating method can be maximized with a big insulated water tank that enables the boiler's hot water to circulate through a heat exchanger to heat the water in the tank.

When the heat is required at night, the hot water from the tank circulates through the heat pipes into the greenhouse. This technique allows for installing a smaller broiler that can be used during the day and at night. Wood-fired boilers also work well with buffer tanks as they absorb the heat from the combustion process and are easy to control, just like fossil fuels.

CONTROLS

Lastly, solid-state controls contribute to greenhouse heating systems. These are accurate heating controls with impactful functions, and water temperature modulation can be added to the boiler system. This system allows for the circulation of lower temperature water through radiation because the greenhouse heat needs to decrease in the daytime.

The control system also reduces overheating by saving energy and adjusting the water temperature based on outdoor temperature and weather conditions. This process also helps the grower save fuel in hot weather.

Additionally, you can heat your greenhouse using wasted hot water from power plants if the plants are close-by. You can also use geothermal heat, which entails hot water being pumped from the ground to the surface to heat the greenhouse. Remember that the aim of setting up the heating system is to ensure that you strike a balance in the temperature of your greenhouse.

As such, your monitoring and close observation of the system are crucial to ascertain if the heating method you chose is working well for you.

CAN A GREENHOUSE BECOME TOO HOT FOR SAFETY?

You already know how important it is to regulate your greenhouse temperature, but can the greenhouse become too hot to be safe? The answer is YES! If direct sunlight enters the greenhouse from the south or west excessively, you will most likely be overheating your plants because the sun's rays' intensity will be too much for them. As such, bright sunshine can overheat the greenhouse even during the winter. This is why bigger commercial greenhouses utilize digital controls to open and close vents as the temperature fluctuates. Moreover, in addition to digital controls, you also have to check the health of your plants. This is why greenhouses, both large and small, should have vents that allow the hot air to escape at the top so cold air can come in from the openings below or on the sides.

In addition to being too hot for plants, an overheated greenhouse can be unsafe for you to work in. Prolonged exposure to excessive heat can cause physical distress, including dehydration and sunstroke.

Now that you fully understand the role of heating systems and some of the options you can choose from let's learn more about water and irrigation.

Chapter - 10
THE DIFFERENCE BETWEEN A GREENHOUSE AND A POLYTUNNEL/LOOP, AND WHICH IS BEST FOR YOUR NEEDS

HOW TO DECIDE?

If you've been growing your fruit and vegetables and are looking for ways to improve your crop, you might consider investing in a poly-tunnel or greenhouse. Protecting harsh weather conditions and many pests could be perfect for extending the growing season, but which alternative do you choose?

This guide discusses the distinctions between poly-tunnels and greenhouses, as well as several factors that need to be considered when making your decision. Do you want to know which one is best for both your growing needs and your garden? Read on to find out about it!

POLY-TUNNELS AND PLASTIC GREENHOUSES

WHAT IS THE DIFFERENCE?

Essentially, both systems function similarly, providing a warmer climate to promote growth during the summer and allow low-temperature plants to survive in the winter. This will help you grow a greater variety of crops (including more Mediterranean crops), in larger numbers and more extended periods. But what are the significant differences?

Poly-tunnels are made of galvanized steel hoops and are tightly linked with transparent or diffused material. Cheaper to buy, poly-tunnels require a smaller investment; at only one-third of the cost of a greenhouse, poly-tunnels are excellent value for money. They are typically constructed directly on the soil base, with a simple site clearance necessary for the site's preparation. They're also easier to dismantle, move and reassemble. The galvanized steel frame will last for 20 years and more, and polythene generally needs to be replaced every 7 to 10 years. Poly-tunnels are available with a full range of additions and accessories to allow you to customize them to meet the specific needs of you and your plants.

Picture of a polytunnel.

Greenhouses use an aluminum or metal frame made of glass or polycarbonate plastic. This can be costly, particularly if you choose toughened safety glass (recommended for family gardens or homes with young

children). Greenhouses are often time-consuming to build, usually requiring a firm foundation to stand on, and once built, they are difficult to disassemble. On the other hand, they are hard-wearing and durable.

Whatever you choose, options may be ideal, especially if you are new to growing your fruit and vegetables and are interested in becoming more self-sufficient.

A small poly-tunnel or greenhouse can be assembled relatively quickly; it is perfect for growing popular plants and can be a great way to get kids into gardening. Also, they are a perfect choice for smaller outdoor areas, from yards to crowded city gardens.

BIG POLY-TUNNEL OR LARGE PLASTIC GREENHOUSE

A large poly-tunnel or large plastic greenhouse is an excellent choice for those who need more space whether it's because you're a more experienced gardener and want to increase your crop variety or require extra space for a commercial venture.

Whatever the cause, a larger size will allow you to take your growth to the level, both for personal use and professional use.

FACTORS TO CONSIDER

When choosing between these two structures and selecting the scale, consider the following considerations:

1. **Purchase Price:** Poly-tunnels are usually cheaper and need less investment than greenhouses.
2. **Construction Time:** Depending on the scale, it can take longer to create the greenhouses.
3. **Site Preparation:** The soil must be level for a greenhouse, while the rougher ground can be more easily accommodated for a poly-tunnel.
4. **Lifespan:** Greenhouses will theoretically last a lifetime, given that the glass does not break or blow out of the frame. Simultaneously, poly-tunnel covers may need to be replaced regularly, at a low cost, to preserve their performance.
5. **Heat Retention:** Greenhouses also need more heat during the winter months, while a poly-tunnel covered with thermal polythene and without a greenhouse design may help if you consider over-wintering crops.
6. **Light and Shades:** Diffused polythene sheeting on a poly-tunnel helps prevent heat spots, but you can need to paint greenhouse panels to avoid sun damage, such as leaf scorch.

7. **Transportability:** While both can be moved, greenhouses take more time, and glass panels may pose a higher risk of damage and injury.

Essentially, your preference will be based on your budget and specifications. However, we hope that these tips will help you choose the right through choice for your needs.

Chapter - 11
UNDERSTANDING THE FERTILIZER LEVEL - PART 1

FERTILIZING YOUR INDOOR GARDEN

Human beings need to drink and eat. When we consider watering, it is clear that plants also need to drink lots of fluids. But as it so happens, plants also need to eat. Only they need their nutrients to come from the soil or liquid fertilizer. The roots of your plants stretch out underneath the soil, spreading in order to seek out more food to provide all the nutrients that they need to keep growing nice and healthy. If you are raising your plants in the ground outdoors, then those roots can stretch a good distance and find lots of nutrients. But when you raise those same plants indoors, there is only so much space in each container that they can spread out, and there are only so many nutrients in the soil. To make certain your indoor plants eat their fill, you need to fertilize them on a regular basis.

Regardless of what potting soil you decide to use, your plants will suck it dry of nutrients in less than two months. When this happens, they will begin to starve. You can buy time in this process by adding a slow-release fertilizer or manure pellets (such as chicken) into the soil. However, these are only going to buy your plants a certain amount of breathing space. They won't be enough on their own to keep your plants from starving. For that, you are going to need to create a schedule to feed your plants a liquid fertilizer regularly. There are many liquid fertilizers available on the market that you can purchase, or you can make your own. We'll see how to make our own in a moment, but before we do, it is a good idea to understand what exactly a fertilizer is providing for your plants. By gaining knowledge of this, you have the best possible understanding of what they require.

The majority of fertilizers available are primarily focused on providing three nutrients to your plants: nitrogen, phosphorus, and potassium, or NPK. I say most fertilizers because there are a decent amount on the market that focuses on only one of these three nutrients rather than all three. You can also purchase these nutrients on their own in a solid form meant to be dissolved in water. However, if you are purchasing pre-made fertilizer for your indoor garden, then the best idea is to choose a fertilizer that has an NPK ratio

with equal amounts of each nutrient. Of course, it is rare that it is always a one-for-one ratio, and so it is okay for the ratio to be a little uneven so long as the nutrients are present in approximately equal quantities. If you are growing fruit or plants that fruit such as strawberries, raspberries, or peppers, then you are going to want to use a fertilizer with a higher amount of potassium as this helps the plants to grow their fruits properly. When using a store-bought fertilizer, you should always follow the instructions on the package so that you avoid overfeeding. When you overfeed them, the pH level in the soil rises to high levels. If you bought soil testing kits or an electronic pH reader, then you should keep a close eye on the pH level.

Buying fertilizer can quickly become expensive if you have a large garden to maintain. One way around this rising cost is to make your own. But be aware that it is always a very smelly process! One way to quickly get yourself some fertilizer is to fill a bag up with compost and let it soak in water for ten days. On day ten, you add water to the mixture until the color changes from black to slightly gray like tea, at which point it is ready to use. Another simple fertilizer uses urine as the primary ingredient since it is sterile, has a decent amount of potassium, and a lot of nitrogen in it, plus it's very easy to acquire because you can use your own! Dilute one part urine with forty parts water, and you have yourself a quick and efficient fertilizer. However, although this method is a little more difficult, you may be interested in making a comfrey fertilizer due to its high potassium concentration. The same steps you take to make a comfrey fertilizer can be used to make a nettle or a borage fertilizer if you need a higher nitrogen count.

Comfrey is a herb from Europe that has high levels of potassium, phosphorus, and nitrogen. That means this one herb can provide you with all the NPK you need from a fertilizer. There are ways to turn this into a fine fertilizer, but it's necessary to note that comfrey is really great because you can grow it yourself. It is pretty much one of the best investments you can make when it comes to feeding your plants. When there is too much carbon in a plant bed, this can make it hard for the plants to get the best benefits from the nitrogen in the soil. Comfrey has a carbon-nitrogen ratio that is perfect in preventing any of these issues.

To make fertilizer out of comfrey, all you need to do is stuff a bunch of comfrey leaves into a large container. It takes a few weeks to start producing this black liquid, though it can be sped up by using a heavy object to press down on the leaves. This liquid is excellent for fertilizer when you mix it with water in a 15:1 ratio. That's all it takes to make comfrey fertilizer, but there is more you can do with comfrey around your garden. Take the leaves out after the pressing and use them to feed your potatoes or as a nutritious mulch. As long as you let comfrey leaves wilt for a few days first, it can be used in this manner. You can also add comfrey leaves to the containers you are planning to use to add more nutrients to the initial soil. Make sure you are using it with slightly older plants and not young seedlings, as it can be too strong for them and lead to nutrient burn. Finally, you can add comfrey leaves to your compost to help make it more nutritious.

If you purchased your fertilizer, then it will have instructions on how often to use it, and you should always listen to these instructions. However, if you have created your own, then you are going to need to educate yourself on the needs of the particular plants you are looking to feed. Some, such as fruiting veggies like or

peppers, will benefit from a weekly feeding schedule. However, there are others which don't need regular fertilizer feed. You should always research your plants before seeding them by either Googling the information or asking your local garden center employees. Also, you shouldn't try to give fertilizer to plants that are overly stressed out. While it may seem like a good idea to dose them with fertilizer to help them get better, it is actually much less stressful for the plant to be given clean water instead. You also won't need to use liquid fertilizer on your herbs, as they generally grow best by being light on nutrients.

The light source must be kept as low as possible in the early stages. When the light is too far away from the seeds, the stems reach the sun and become vulnerable and delicate. The amount of light required every day varies, but the rule of thumb is 14-16 hours a day. Soil temperature is essential, not room temperature, and your seed packets should be kept as recommended. Most plants do best between 70-80 degrees, but the temperature of choice varies. Control the watering again. The soil should not be soggy. When the first seedling leaves begin to appear, properly called cotyledons, the plastic dome should be removed. You should start fertilizing when your baby plants grow their second set of leaves. Continue feeding once a week using a half-strength liquid plant starter fertilizer.

MAKING THE MOST OF COMPOST

Your greenhouse will be in high demand for nutrient-dense dirt. Decent topsoil and quality compost will be your best tools in the greenhouse. But you'll be going through a lot. Your best bet will be to gather compost and reuse it as much as possible. You can make your own by capturing any plant waste leftover in your greenhouse after harvest.

There are several methods of generating compost, but the most effective for small-scale greenhouses is a compost bin. You can incorporate a simple compost bin into your construction by building it near your greenhouse, or you can purchase a small barrel-style composter.

The media for your compost is right in your own backyard. After harvest, be sure to save up your rootstock, leafy plants, and wood chips if you have them. You'll want to make sure they are in equal portions and free from disease, insects, and harmful chemicals. When you are ready to plant, you can extract from the compost and refill the pots.

Compost also generates small amounts of heat as the material inside decomposes. If you are struggling to maintain adequate heat in your greenhouse during the winter months, you may be able to add a compost bin inside to bump the temperature a little. If you struggle with excessive heat, be sure to keep your compost bins a fair distance away from your greenhouse.

Chapter - 12
LEARN HOW TO HEAT YOUR GREENHOUSE AND USE VENTILATION TO KEEP THE HUMIDITY LEVEL JUST RIGHT

Controlling the temperatures within the greenhouse is essential for your crops' survival. Let's look at each of the following conditions and how you can regulate them and maximize your produce.

HEATING

Once you set up the greenhouse, you need to keep the temperature of the greenhouse between 80° to 85°F (27° to 29°C). During the day, the greenhouse harnesses heat energy from the sun's rays and uses it to heat the garden's internal air. You can also get heat from other sources like electric heaters or gas.

A hot water boiler is highly recommended as a heating system. Water temperature should be regulated to satisfy the needs of each heating system. Depending on the specific crop's needs, each greenhouse should have independent temperature control.

Any of these heat sources can quickly heat the structure to higher temperatures of over 100°F (40°C), which can kill your crops. Therefore, you need to regulate the interior temperature to a range of 80° to 85°F (27° to 30°C).

VENTILATION AND AIR FLOW

When designing a greenhouse, you must include vents either at the rooftop with a hatch you can open on the ceiling or have side vents. Plants need carbon dioxide (CO2) to grow and release oxygen (O2) and moisture into the environment. You need good ventilation in the area to avoid growing crops under humid conditions.

Fans will be a great addition for cooling the environment, as they can whisk out the hot air and introduce cooler air inside. You can choose to operate the vents either manually or automatically. If you install manual vents, make sure you open them every day and close them at night.

If you're on a budget, the manual vent system can work for you as long as you will always be available to open and close it as the weather changes. If you're not always around, maintaining a manual vent system may be difficult for you; therefore, an automated system would be the best alternative.

An automatic ventilation system uses a sensor programmed to automatically turn on the fans or the heating system when temperatures change. The sensors monitor temperatures when they rise and fall and automatically switch the fans and heaters on or off. This ensures constant air circulation and cooling of the greenhouse structure.

During the warmer days, you can ensure enough ventilation by opening the door to your garden. Make sure to put a heavy rock on the door or tie it to prevent wind from shutting it. If the structure is made of cold frames, you can also open the lid to allow more air to circulate inside during the day.

LIGHTING

To control the light levels, you need to have a shade cloth in either green or any other dark color. You can place the material on all the windows on the outside of the greenhouse, and you can also roll it up and down to adjust the temperatures inside. This material will act a shade and prevent an excess of light from entering through the windows.

The shade cloth is crucial during the summer months. It helps in regulating heat and cooling the greenhouse temperatures while allowing moderate light inside the structure. During the winter months, you can roll the cloth up to allow more light to enter inside.

HUMIDITY

The amount of humidity present in your garden is essential in determining your vegetables' survival. You must keep the garden environment humid at all times and at least ensure you have a humidity of 50% or higher.

Benches are great for keeping moisture away. A bench is a type of table with lips at the edge, and it is used to hold plants in place. Wooden benches have a tray inserted to keep moisture away from the wood, whereas metal benches have a mesh top attached to them to make it easy to drain water and moisture.

HOW TO KEEP THE GREENHOUSE WARM

1. USING BUBBLE WRAP TO INSULATE THE GREENHOUSE

Insulating a greenhouse garden with a bubble wrap will ensure heat doesn't escape away. For better insulation, buy a wrap with bigger bubbles. You should also cover all doors and windows to ensure heat doesn't escape, especially during the winter. This practice will not only keep the greenhouse warm, but will also reduce the cost of heating.

2. USING HEATERS

A small heater added to the greenhouse can help regulate the greenhouse's temperature, especially during the night. The plants can use the heater's carbon dioxide and convert it to oxygen, which is essential for humans.

The cold weather outside will not affect your plants inside the greenhouse if you have a heater installed.

3. USING AIR CIRCULATORS INSIDE THE GREENHOUSE

Heaters will not be enough to provide warmth inside the greenhouse; you will also have to make sure the fresh air circulated inside the greenhouse is warmed evenly to avoid having cold and hot patches on the plants.

Installing air circulators will ensure there is an even distribution of warm air inside the greenhouse. You can buy an air circulator fan or use the air circulation function from KlimaHeat to mix the air.

If you have no electricity in the area, you can protect the plants from the cold weather by:

1. USING COMPOST

The bacteria that break down organic matter during the composting process, generates heat; therefore, adding more compost to the soil will generate heat that can keep your plants warm.

Add a layer of soil about 3 inches thick to enable the bacteria to create a warm environment for the plant roots.

2. USING A DOUBLE LAYER OF PLASTIC MATERIAL TO MAKE WINDOWS

Insulating the windows can help the greenhouse retain more heat. Although insulation can block the amount of light from entering, using a double layer of insulation material on the windows can add more warmth inside. As a result, you double the R-value (insulation) of the greenhouse.

3. USING BLACK MULCH ON ALL PATHWAYS

The pathways inside the greenhouse or between the planting beds absorb heat. Adding black mulch, or any other dark color mulch, to the pathways will absorb more sunlight and convert it to heat, keeping your plants' roots warm.

4. USING HEAT TO ABSORB BARRELS

Put black barrels in an area where they can have direct access to sunlight, as they will absorb more sunlight and use that to convert heat that will warm the water inside. As it goes, you should place the black plastic barrels in water.

The warm water created will act as thermal mass and hold for a longer period, providing warmth to greenhouse plants.

Although they use sunlight themselves, make sure to place the barrels so that they won't block sunlight from reaching the plants. Barrels work well when placed on the northern corner of the greenhouse. During the summer, you should cover these barrels with a white material to prevent them from creating extra heat in the greenhouse.

5. BUILDING THE GREENHOUSE PARTIALLY UNDERGROUND

Building the greenhouse 4 inches deeper on the ground will help retain more warmth and acts as an insulator against the cold air from outside the structure. During the cold season, the ground will be warm. This provides the warmth needed for the roots of the plant to grow.

If you have a greenhouse building facing the south hillside, it will absorb more heat to warm the ground.

6. UTILIZING THERMAL MASS OBJECTS

Using objects like clay, rocks, and bricks can absorb heat when the air circulating inside is warm and release the absorbed heat when the air inside is cold. Therefore, having raised beds made of clay or brick material can absorb heat and warm the greenhouse. You can boost the amount of warmth released by adding a black barrel to the water inside.

7. INSULATING THE NORTHERN SIDE

If you stay in the Northern hemisphere, there is no need to fix glass on the northern side because the sun doesn't shine on that side. Adding insulators on the northern side will help retain heat inside the greenhouse and prevent north winds from inside. Besides, putting a thermal heating mass on the wall can absorb more sunlight.

Chapter - 13
SECURING YOUR GREENHOUSE AGAINST THE WIND

One of the biggest dangers your greenhouse faces is the wind. High wind can rip a greenhouse to pieces, twisting the frame and shattering the glass, so you need to take steps to protect your precious greenhouse and the plants inside.

Firstly, you need to ensure that all the panes of glass are securely in place and none are broken. A corner missing out of a pane can give the wind ingress to blow out other panes and damage your greenhouse. Although a greenhouse isn't a completely sealed unit, solid panes will protect it from wind damage.

You can buy a galvanized steel base for your greenhouse, which usually comes as a flat pack. Although not essential, these are extremely helpful as the base will raise up your greenhouse a little and make it more stable because you can secure the base to the foundation and the greenhouse.

A greenhouse base is secured to the foundation by pushing specially designed metal hooks into wet concrete pockets secured to the frame. An alternative fixing is to lay a concrete strip that sits under the greenhouse base. Drilling then secures the base as it is bolted to the concrete.

One of the favorite ways to secure a greenhouse is to lay a single course of bricks on a concrete footing and then secure the greenhouse to the bricks without using a greenhouse base.

Of course, you can dramatically reduce the potential for damage simply by locating your greenhouse in a more sheltered area. The trouble is you often have to balance sun exposure with shelter.

Although you can do everything possible to protect your greenhouse, you cannot make it completely stormproof no matter what you do. There will also be cases where a freak storm hits. If severe weather warnings are given for your area, then you should probably remove any plants you want to save to another location where they will be protected during the storm.

If your greenhouse is square and level, then it is more likely to have a better fitting glass. The loose glass will

rattle, and this has much more chance of breaking. The gaps in a non-square frame allow the wind into the greenhouse to cause all sorts of destruction.

Most greenhouses will have a flexible rubber glazing seal between the glass and the aluminum frame. These tend to perish over time and will frequently disappear when moving a greenhouse. These seals hold the glass in place and prevent the wind from getting into your greenhouse. Regularly check your seals and replace them if they start to perish. It will go a long way to protecting your greenhouse from wind damage.

Glazing clips hold the glass to the frame, and these have a habit of vanishing. They pop off during wind storms, get knocked off, and generally vanish. You should check the glazing clips at least once a year to make sure they are in place. If any are missing, then they should be replaced as soon as possible.

Both of these items are relatively cheap and easy to find. You will typically find the best prices online on sites such as eBay.

If high winds or a storm are forecasts, you should make sure that all vents, windows, and doors are shut. Although automatic vents are a wonderful thing, if they open up during a storm, they could end up destroying your greenhouse, so turn them off during storms!

If you live in a particularly windy area, then you may want to consider putting up a windbreak to protect your greenhouse. It may be worthwhile sacrificing some sunshine for protection from the wind.

Siting a greenhouse, so the prevailing wind flows over it rather than hits one end is another method of reducing wind damage potential.

Another option is to replace your horticultural glass with toughened safety glass. This is stronger, so it's harder to break. It comes in larger panes, so you do not have smaller, overlapping panes. Also, toughened glass is much easier to clean up than horticultural glass if there is any damage.

Most greenhouses will use glass clips to hold the glass in place, but you can use bar capping or continuous strip fixings, which are stronger and less likely to give in high winds.

One of your prime considerations when sitting and building your greenhouse has to be to protect it from damage in the wind. A greenhouse is a significant investment in both time and money and should it get wrecked you could lose your seedlings or crops. Before you begin erecting your greenhouse understand the wind patterns in your area and place your greenhouse in the best location you can to reduce the wind's impact.

Chapter - 14
THE BEST WAY TO CLEAN YOUR GREENHOUSE TO COMBAT DISEASE AND PEST

REMOVE BUGS AND PESTS

Wash all the benches in the garden with soapy water. This strategy will enable you to remove dirt and moisture that can cause mold.

Always ensure you keep the greenhouse's surface dry, and you can use a cloth or a sponge to wipe clean any moisture or damp areas on the surface. Spray any built-up mildew on the walls with the mildew spray. You should also clean the area between the panes to avoid the buildup of condensation, leading to molds and algae's growth.

Clean the flooring area of your structure thoroughly. Some floors are made of wood, gravel, cement, or fabric carpeting, and depending on your greenhouse's floor type, molds can grow. You need to scrub the floor and clean out any mold, mud, and other decaying matter.

Remove any dead plant branches and leaves. Pests or bugs can infect plants, causing the leaves to wither, and prune any dead leaves or branches to prevent further disease spread. You must take the dead leaves out of the greenhouse as soon as possible because if left inside, they may decompose and allow pests or bugs into the greenhouse.

Weeds and any other unimportant plants around the greenhouse area should be removed.

If some pests invade your greenhouse, you can release spiders and ladybugs into the garden if they are available in your area. If ladybugs are not available in your pet stores, you can use pesticides to deal with pests in the greenhouse instead.

PROVIDE SHADE AND MORE SUN

Most greenhouse roofs and windows are made of plastic material or fiberglass. These materials can turn a darker shade caused by overheating from the sun or microscopic molds after some time. This change can reduce the amount of light in the greenhouse.

You should periodically clean the windows to allow more light and sun to enter the greenhouse. Consider replacing the roof material after a while.

Plant trees that can provide shade for your greenhouse during the summer months, which can act as shade to protect your plants from hot weather. You should plant the trees on the west side of the greenhouse to block the sun and excess light into the structure. The trees shed off the leaves during the winter, allowing the extra sun to get into the greenhouse.

Alternatively, you can install roll-up shades. Roll-up shades are closed during the summer to protect the plants from the sun and remain opened in winter to allow more sun and light to enter.

HEATING AND VENTILATION PROBLEMS

Greenhouses provide a temperature-controlled environment to meet the needs of your plants. You need to maintain the heating and ventilation equipment and ensure they're working properly. Check the equipment regularly and do full maintenance on them before the winter growing season.

If there are gaps in the greenhouse exterior, you can use new glass panes to fill out the large holes or caulk to fill small holes in the exterior. This ensures you maintain heat inside the greenhouse.

Paint all walls black, as doing so makes sure that you attract and retain more heat.

You can install roof vents between the ceiling and the rooftop. In most greenhouses, hot air is always trapped at the top of the ceiling and prevents the crops from receiving enough warmth. Installing vents can easily push away hot air and allow fresh air from the outside, thus increasing fresh air circulation.

You can also use fans installed diagonally at the opposite corners of the greenhouse, which increase fresh air circulation inside. Switch off the fans in the winter to conserve heat.

You should also consider a watering system or piping system. Make sure you properly install the water system and that it works as desired. You must also do frequent maintenance on the pipes to ensure no leaks.

WEED CONTROL

Weeds growing in the greenhouses and other covered structures are among the most persistent problems that many farmers face. These weeds affect plants' quality, and other types of weeds can act as hosts for pests like whiteflies, snails, mites, and slugs.

Weeds that grow under the benches inside the greenhouse will usually host some pests and fungi; therefore, you need to develop mechanisms to control the weed growth.

Removing the weed from the greenhouse benches, pots, and even the floor is important in managing the greenhouse and maintaining its aesthetic. A ground cloth put under the benches is highly recommended for weed management.

An accumulation of potting media on the ground can appear to act as the perfect environment for weed growth if you do not collect it. A ground cloth can easily collect the spilled potting media and prevent any germination of weed seeds.

Weeds that have already grown under the benches may force you to use herbicide to help manage them. There is a wide variety of herbicides in the market, but most are for outdoor use, while very few are for indoor use. Don't be tempted to buy the ones labeled for use outdoors, as it may have negative effects on the crops grown inside. In extreme cases, it can affect your plants in the season. Vapor from some of the

traditional herbicides can be trapped inside the structure and will not only affect the crops but they could also be a health hazard to the people working in the greenhouse.

When applying greenhouse herbicides on the benches, read the instructions carefully. There are two types of herbicides in the greenhouse: Pre-emergence activity and Marengo. You can apply the herbicide labeled "pre-emergency activity" when the crop is present, and you can water the plant pot even after application. You should not apply BareSpot herbicides on the pot.

You cannot use Marengo herbicide when the plant is present; instead, apply Marengo herbicide before the start of the growing season. Watering the area with the applied herbicide activates its residual compound, which can damage plants in the area due to volatilization from the herbicide.

PREVENTION MEASURES

You should come up with a weed management program that allows you to regularly monitor the potting, plant holding, propagation, and the surrounding areas for the presence of weeds.

Before removing the weeds, identify the weed type, its life cycle, and the area where it's growing. Always make sure to manually remove weeds from the pots and benches after the plant's flower and produce seeds.

The best weed control measure is through weed sanitation; that is, keeping away any weed propagules (like seeds and rhizomes) in the greenhouse structure by using sterile media and cleaning plant materials. You should also control weeds growing outside the greenhouse.

Building concrete floors or having mulched floors will limit weed growth on the floors.

You can manually pull the weeds and prevent them from reaching the seed area in the greenhouse too. Mow the outside to control the weeds outdoors.

Use weed block fabric, which will act as a physical barrier to prevent weed establishment on the floor or under the benches.

You should also use weed-free potting soil. If the container or planting pots spill the potting media, clean them.

In areas where weeds continue to be a problem, you can remove the soil in that area or cover the area with mulch to prevent the weeds' growth.

WEED MANAGEMENT

Managing the weed growing conditions is essential for every greenhouse. A weed-free environment reduces the need for pesticides and increases the production of high-quality crops. Proper weed control practices help keep pests, insects, and weed diseases at bay.

Weeds compete with your crops for light, water, and nutrients; therefore, you should remove them as soon as possible before they affect your crops' growth. These weeds carry their own viruses too, which can damage or infect your crops.

A weed management program will help you manage and control the weeds in your greenhouse effectively while helping you develop control measures.

SOURCES OF WEED SEEDS

Weeds come from a variety of sources, some of which include:

- Ventilation fans blowing weed seeds from outside into the greenhouse.
- Contaminated seeds.
- Infected plants transplanted in the greenhouse from an external source.
- Poor plant growing area and storage or using dirty pots and containers.
- Contaminated or uncovered soil from under tables and benches.
- From the irrigation systems and water ponds.

Chapter - 15
AN OVERVIEW OF THE ESSENTIAL EQUIPMENT YOU NEED TO KEEP YOUR GARDEN HEALTHY

Greenhouse equipment is built in the most accurate manner; this segment contains numerous brands that supply world-class goods. Such goods are checked several times before they are released on the market to give you a hint. What distinguishes them is the quality at hand; if you choose a premium brand, this can certainly give you the required performance. Now, coming to the selection portion, this is the first step towards the main building. You are advised to choose well and to suit your needs. One wrong move, and in the building process, everything can go wrong. You also need to work on small details that can deliver the best output for you. There may be information about the greenhouse's design and other safety features.

Greenhouse equipment is made up of watering, lighting, exhausts, windows, and other construction equipment. Buying all of this in the right way will help to save time and costs. Digital shopping can be considered a good choice for your needs. There are times where buying online will certainly give you all the long-term benefits. Each brand that the supplier's equipment has its website, you can search on their website for greenhouse equipment and then finalize your vision. Price comparison can be made online, online purchases, and quotations from the internet can be used for price comparison. Selecting the right products, will give you an added advantage.

Just know the brand you want to buy through; it should have consumer credibility. One should not go ahead without testing the brand as you may not know the type of service provided. Check on the website for customer evaluation, and this should give you an indication of the type of customer service offered.

Greenhouse equipment should be produced in compliance with international standards; if the product complies with local standards, then the reliability and overall stability factor are expected to decrease. It would also help to make the order easy and affordable by looking for free delivery options. You don't need to waste time arranging for the purchased products to be transported. When it comes to such goods, choose wisely.

Therefore, buying greenhouse equipment is proving beneficial in the long run. With such equipment and tools, your dream greenhouse can be installed in no time. Make sure you have full permission from your greenhouse building architect. Beautify your landscape with state-of-the-artist greenhouses.

BUILDING GREENHOUSES ACCESSORIES WORTH HAVING

Greenhouses are typically a practical operation, but that doesn't mean that they just need to be functional. A lot of optional components can be added to a greenhouse to make it more comfortable and more functional. Read on and learn about the extras that can greatly improve your greenhouse. These are truly worth making greenhouse accessories.

An adjustable irrigation system is the first among the "key" greenhouse accessories. You can do this through overhead sprinklers or water feeds at the soil level. The main reason for this is to boost water distribution to all the plants, and the problem often requires a lot of effort. If you are able to swing an automated computer system, that's even better! So, you can make the watering routine and just let it do its job.

Sturdy racks are highly recommended for those who want to grow plants in their greenhouse pots. Racks multiply the area on which you can grow plants so that you can add more plant biomass to your controlled system. It also makes things on your knees and back much easier, raising the need to pause or squat down to accomplish tasks. Make sure your racks are using rustproof and rot-proof materials, or you might face catastrophic failure.

It's nice to have a water pressurizer and a long nozzle-equipped pipeline. Not for plants to drink, although that can be done. Be patient, however, when doing so, as the pressure can crush or rip the plants apart. Cleaning is the key reason for having a mobile system with a pressurized water supply. It will make it much easier to clean your greenhouse, particularly for roof panels to be cleaned. Through climbing onto the roof, you will not have to take risks this way—just lean a ladder on the greenhouse side, ascend, and blast away.

It's a good idea to install a ventilation system in your greenhouse. Plants can wilt under excess heat, so you're going to need a way out into the greenhouse to cycle cool air. This is an emergency measure and can delete any discoveries you have made, but it can save the plants, which is better than starting from scratch. A chest or cabinet that is waterproof is a perfect place to store your equipment in the greenhouse. This will protect them against rust damage and moisture while reducing the need to move in and out of the greenhouse—behavior that will risk the greenhouse's temperature and health.

Have a few large sheets of plastic on hand to patch broken panes. Such temporary measures will keep the conditions of your greenhouse in check until you have a replacement stand. As you can see, a lot of things can be used to boost a greenhouse's functionality. There are things that we sometimes take for granted, which eventually give us a lot of support. You need to plan when constructing greenhouses to accommodate

additional features, such as those shown above.

Building and running a greenhouse can be more than just a fun recreational activity you do in your spare time–it can help you financially (if you sell plants or produce) and safely (by eating healthy foods). Installing such main accessories will ensure that your greenhouse will provide you with maximum return and performance.

Vegetation thrives when the growth area, climate, and disease and pest protection factors are maintained at optimum rates. Accessories make it easier and quicker to know and manage these optimal conditions. These come at a high cost, but they may well be worth the returns.

HERE ARE SOME USEFUL GREENHOUSE ACCESSORIES TO HAVE

Heaters: heaters are the first greenhouse equipment you need to install in your greenhouse. This is because plants need to thrive at a specific temperature. This is particularly important if your greenhouse for plastic or glass is located in a cold area that gets colder during winter. The heaters come in many types as per your specifications, such as gas heaters, paraffin heaters, or electric heaters. It is important to avoid blowing air directly on plants, and however, as it can be harmful, it is always beneficial for the heat (or cool air) at the level of the soil.

Climate controls: Climate controls are also critical greenhouse devices, just like heaters. Depending on the season, a good climate control system can heat up or cool the greenhouse. It is recommended that you position your plants on benches so that even air circulation is provided. Heating and cooling thermostats, variable speed controls, humidistat, cycle timers, and advanced controls are the various types of controls available on the market.

Ventilation equipment: As the name suggests, this device helps manage the air in your garden so you can grow plants that usually don't thrive in your area. Choose from any of the following greenhouse ventilation devices, such as evaporative coolers, exhaust fans & shutters, automatic vent openers, and circulation fans, for proper air circulation in your greenhouse environment.

Misting Systems: Effective misting systems are useful in any greenhouse construction process to maintain optimal humidity and temperature, ensuring plants grow at the desired rate. There is a wide range of options such as sprinkler systems, misting systems, mist timers & valves, and water filters that are commonly used in institutional greenhouse-style installations.

Watering supplies: as is obvious, water supplies are the most important part to take care of even during the greenhouse design. From a wide range of water supplies such as plant watering systems, drip systems, qualified water hoses, water timers, and overhead watering systems, you can choose according to your specific requirements.

Irrigation system: Without water, plants cannot grow. An irrigation system will make it easier to distribute water to the greenhouse plants quickly and evenly. Combining customizable nozzles, overhead sprinklers, and field drip feeders would be the perfect irrigation method.

Downpipe kits: You can save considerable watering costs by collecting the runoff of rainwater. Downpipe kits harness rainwater that will channel it to reservoirs and later feed into the greenhouse's irrigation and/or cooling system. The only catch is to ensure that the water is purified from soil or debris before being pumped into the irrigation or cooling system, as this may cause a blockage.

Greenhouse shelving: If you put in your backyard a greenhouse, space is likely to be a major constraint. Greenhouse shelves ensure that the vertical area is used as much as possible. Shelving comes in various heights, a number of shelves, and construction material.

Growing racks: Growing racks ensure a mini greenhouse is used effectively and easily. The racks shield plants from extreme weather impacts, while the zippers allow access to the seedlings.

Shade cloth: Shades shield the plants from the sun's harmful ultraviolet rays and help regulate the greenhouse temperature. The shades can be manual or controlled by the sensor. For areas where sunlight and outside temperatures typically change rapidly, manual shades can be complicated.

Vent openers: Reduce heating and air conditioning cost by installing winds at suitable locations. You can choose between natural and automatic ventilation, which is costly but more efficient and can be built into central heating or air conditioning system.

Chapter - 16

HOW TO IRRIGATE YOUR GREENHOUSE TO AUTOMATICALLY WATER YOUR PLANT AND PROTECT THEM FROM HEAT DAMAGE

The main issue you will face with a greenhouse is keeping your plants watered. In hot weather, they can dry out very quickly, and this can cause problems such as leaf, flower, or fruit drop, which you obviously want to avoid.

If your greenhouse is in your garden then it is easy enough to pop down and water it, but if it is at an allotment or you are on holiday then watering becomes much trickier, putting your harvest at risk.

In the hottest weather, and more so in hotter climates, you will need to water your plants two or three times a day to keep them healthy no matter how good your cooling system is!

Although you can hand-water the plants in your greenhouse, this can soon get boring and difficult to keep up. The best and most effective way to water plants is to invest in greenhouse irrigation systems. The choice depends on the size of the greenhouse, the plants being grown, and the availability of electricity and water.

If you are planning to irrigate your greenhouse, then the need to be sited near to water and/or electricity can heavily influence your choice of location.

There are a lot of different irrigation systems on the market with widely varying prices, so you do need to spend some time considering your requirements before rushing out to buy one.

Other plants require more water than others, so depending on what you are growing, you may want to get an automatic irrigation system that can deliver differing quantities of water to different plants.

You also want a system that can grow with you as you put more plants in your greenhouse. At certain times within the season, you will have more plants in your greenhouse, so your irrigation system needs to be able to support this extra demand.

You need to be careful because any irrigation system that is introducing too much water to your greenhouse could make it too damp, which will encourage the growth of diseases. This is one reason you need to have your drainage and ventilation right to prevent your greenhouse ecosystem damage.

You typically have two choices about how to deliver water to your plants, either through spray heads or a drip system. The former will spray water over everything in your greenhouse. The downside of this is that it can encourage powdery mildew on certain plants, but the spray can help damp down your greenhouse. It can also be a bit hit and miss how much ends up in your plants' soil. If you are growing in containers, then a spray system may not deliver water precisely enough.

Drip systems though, will deliver water precisely to containers and give each container exactly the right amount of water, so no plant goes thirsty!

Most irrigation systems present downsides because they require electricity, which can be difficult, expensive, or even impossible for some greenhouse owners to install. You can purchase solar-powered irrigation systems, which will do the job, but they can struggle on duller days.

The water will come into the greenhouse with piping, and correctly locating this is important. Hanging it from the ceiling and running it along the walls helps keep it out of the way and stops it from getting damaged. Running the piping along the floor is a recipe for disaster as you are bound to end up putting a container on it and damaging it!

You will need a water supply and ideally mains water, but you can run some irrigation systems from water butts. You will have to check regularly that the water butt has enough water in it, but it is still much easier than manually watering your plants!

OVERHEAD MISTERS

If you grow mostly or all one type of plant, then an overhead watering method is a great choice because you can water all your plants evenly and easily. For larger greenhouses, this is a great system because it will water a large area quickly.

The downside of this system is that it is quite wasteful of water because the water goes everywhere in the greenhouse, not just into the containers where your plants are.

Your plants end up getting a lot of water on their leaves. If they are over-crowded or ventilation is poor, then this can cause problems such as powdery mildew and make your plants more susceptible to disease.

MAT IRRIGATION

You can buy capillary matting, which works as an irrigation system for your plants. This is a special mat that is designed to draw up water which your plants then absorb through moisture wicks which go into the soil of your containers.

The mat is kept moist by a drip watering system, so you do not have to run water piping throughout your greenhouse. It can just go to strategic points where it feeds the capillary matting.

This is a relatively cheap method of irrigation and is very simple to install. The big advantage is it is very efficient in its use of water, and there is little risk of overwatering your plants!

DRIP TUBING

This is special tubing that you run throughout your greenhouse. It has tubes attached to it that run to each container's roots to supply water directly to the soil. The big advantage of most drip systems is that you can control the amount of water dripped into your plants. This means that plants that need more water can get it, and plants that need less don't get over-watered.

This is set to drip at a certain rate or to operate on a timer, so it waters at regular intervals. It will depend on the type of system you buy as to whether it is constant or timed. Timed is by far the best as it allows greater control of water delivery, reducing the risks of over-watering.

This is a very water-efficient method of watering your greenhouse with minimal wastage. It can also be set up to be completely automatic, which reduces the time you spend managing your greenhouse.

With some of the more advanced drip watering systems, you have sensors in the ground that monitor moisture levels and turn on the water when the soil becomes too dry.

If you are growing directly in the soil, then the soil type will influence your drip-rate. A heavy clay soil will take longer to absorb water, so it needs less water than lighter soil because, in clay, it will puddle and pool, which you want to avoid.

When you grow various plants, this is by far the best irrigation method because you can control the amount of water each container receives.

Planning your drip watering system is relatively easy. You need to divide your greenhouse into an equal number of s, and each area will hold plants with similar water requirements. Depending on your greenhouse size, you may need multiple irrigation systems, but most are easy to expand with additional piping.

Drip irrigation piping comes in either black polyethylene (PE) or polyvinyl chloride (PVC). These are cheap, easy to handle, and bendy when you need them to be.

PVC pipe is often used in supply and header lines as you can solvent bond connections and fittings. Polyethylene connections though, need to be clamped. PVC pipe is also more durable, being less sensitive to temperature fluctuations and sunlight, but it is more expensive to buy.

Polyethylene pipe is sensitive to high temperatures and will contract and expand. This means it can move out of position unless it is held in place.

Your main feeder piping may be 1" or 2" wide emitters, lines ½" piping is sufficient. Each row of plants will have its own ½" line containing emitters. In smaller greenhouses, you can get away with one emitter line for every two rows when plants are spaced less than 18-20" apart.

There are some different types of emitters available. The perforated hose or porous pipe types are very common and are an emitter line with holes in them. The water then seeps out of these holes. Most will deliver water at a rate of anywhere from ½ to 3 gallons an hour. The rate of delivery is changed by adjusting the water pressure.

Alternatively, you can get emitter valves that allow you to control the drip rate for each pot.

Emitters are usually spaced between 24" and 36" along the main lines.

One thing to remember is that you need to filter the water, particularly if it is coming out of a water butt. This prevents dust from entering the system and blocking the transmitter. This is vital as it will ensure your irrigation system works without any problems.

Some irrigation systems will allow you to install a fertilizer injector. This is useful as you can get your irrigation system to feed your plants too automatically! Depending on the system, this can be set to deliver liquid fertilizer constantly or at specified intervals. This, though, is typically found in more expensive systems, and you need to be very careful in your choice of liquid feed to prevent clogging up the system.

The key with drip irrigation systems is to apply a little water frequently to maintain the soil moisture levels. This is a very water-efficient system that is easy to expand and works no matter what size plants you are growing.

Most people who own a greenhouse and install an irrigation system will choose a drip watering system. They are easily available and very affordable though, as with anything, you can spend more money and get more advanced systems.

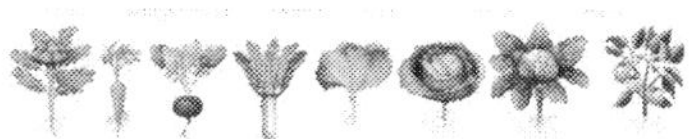

Chapter - 17
HOW TO PREPARE YOUR GREENHOUSE FOR THE GROWING SEASON

Your crop production can be significantly accelerated through the use of a greenhouse control or automation system. With this type of environmental regulation, the greenhouse remains constant to provide optimal conditions that are most favorable for maximum yield.

The management of the greenhouse environment aims to maximize the photosynthetic cycle of plants and the ability of plants to use light at optimum output.

LIGHTING CONTROL

There's a lot more to the decoration of the greenhouse that meets the eye. Growers looking for suitable lighting for their greenhouse should consider the following three factors: the type of crop being cultivated, the time of year, and the amount of sunlight available.

Greenhouses generally require six hours of direct or full-spectrum light per day. If this cannot be done naturally, additional lighting must be included. Additional lighting is the use of multiple, high-intensity artificial lights to encourage crop growth and yield.

Growers have a wide variety of lighting choices to choose from, so it is necessary to understand different lighting types complexities. Again, this is made easier to handle with greenhouse environmental restrictions that can be prepared and tracked.

HUMIDITY CONTROL

As plants begin to increase their growth rate, you may want to will moisture gradually to promote transpiration, allowing more water to flow through the plant.

Humidity should also be controlled carefully because if it gets too hot in the greenhouses, plant leaves

have a much higher chance of being wet. Sadly, damp leaves are one of the easiest ways to allow a fungal infection or a mildew outbreak. Fungal diseases such as Botrytis pathogen or powdery mildew are natural causes of greenhouse disease. Controlling and monitoring the greenhouse ecosystem ensures greater quality management.

VENTILATION & FAN CONTROL

The use of vents is another simple way to help control temperature and humidity. Through the use of rack and pinion and ventilation control, if it begins to get too hot, the greenhouse vents can be opened at a fixed temperature.

Horizontal airflow fans with greenhouse control systems can also be triggered. These increase air circulation and help to extract moisture from the air. To maintain a proper balance, it is essential to increase greenhouse temperatures.

With proper greenhouse temperature and humidity sensors, all of this is controlled by our greenhouse automation machine. This will help you track and control the humidity and temperature levels more effectively. A grower-approved greenhouse environmental control program ensures that all rates are kept in check.

CARBON DIOXIDE OR CO2 CONTROL

Supplying a lot of carbon dioxide to your plants is essential for healthy plant production. Plants take carbon from the environment as a necessary part of photosynthesis. Through the stomata openings, carbon dioxide enters the plant through the diffusion cycle.

CO2 increases productivity by increasing plant growth and overall health. Some forms in which CO2 productivity is increased include earlier flowering, higher fruit yields, and longer growth cycles.

Going into some of the more advanced calculations here, but for most greenhouse crops, net photosynthesis increases as CO2 levels rise from 340–1,000 ppm (parts per million).

Most of the crops show that, for any given level of active photosynthetic radiation (PAR), increasing the level of CO2 to 1,000 ppm would increase photosynthesis by about 50% above the level of ambient CO2.

Stay within the quality control guidelines of our greenhouse climate control system to control the CO2 ranges properly.

AIR TEMPERATURE CONTROL

The increase in air temperature will increase the rate of photosynthesis to a point. However, above 85 degrees, the plants go into photorespiration. Plants can begin to wither, which is not ideal for growing.

If you do not balance higher air temperatures with higher levels of carbon dioxide and light intensity, your plants will do more photorespiration than photosynthesis, which will have an immense impact on the health of your plants.

At some stage, enzymes will not perform their functions and will fall apart, and your plants will not develop a healthy metabolism. Balance with a greenhouse temperature control system is essential in all aspects.

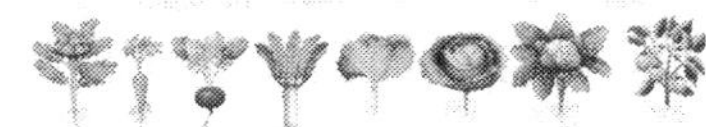

Chapter - 18
SCHEDULING YOUR PLANTING THROUGHOUT THE YEAR

The goal of a greenhouse is to keep things growing year-round, right? How do you ensure you do that? You have to come up with a planting schedule, and for that, you have to consider two things. One is the temperature, and the second is the day length.

Day length is likely the most important factor in determining when you should plant something in your greenhouse. If you don't plan on using supplemental lighting, it will be critical for you to know how long your days are for your area year-round. This is going to vary greatly depending on if you live in a Northern area or Southern area. It can also be affected by living in the mountains or the valleys. For the most part, February marks when the days and nights start to become equal, and the amount of sunlight during the day will start to grow from there until around November. Remember, though, this might not be true for you, especially if you live in New York, Oregon, Pennsylvania, and other similar states. Their days are still pretty short at that time. However, if you live in Nevada, Arizona, or certain parts of California, your days could be longer than your nights. Please, keep this in mind and come up with your schedule based on your city. The planting schedule we will go over is an average, and you can adjust it to fit your local climate.

GROWING GUIDE AND PLANTING SCHEDULE

A planting schedule isn't just knowing what plants to plant when. It also involves the workings of the greenhouse. If you want to plant all year, maintenance goes into keeping your greenhouse running smoothly. In our planting schedule, which you can adjust to your needs, we will also go over important maintenance that you will need to keep up during the year.

- **JANUARY**

This is a pretty quiet time during the growing season. It provides you the best opportunity to give your greenhouse the once over and make sure that everything is functioning as it should, especially if your greenhouse is on the older side.

As for your plants, feed the spring-flowering bulbs, like narcissus, crocus, and hyacinth. Store polyanthus and pot-grown inside. This is the time to take cuttings from chrysanthemums. Put rooted seedlings, like pelargonium, in pots. You can sow some bedding plants in a heated propagator, such as carnations, verbena, and lobelia. You can early plant potatoes for cropping in May.

- **FEBRUARY**

You will likely need to start watering more often; just make sure that the soil is not overwatered. Keep an eye on frosty weather and keep your temperature constant. You need to cover tender plants and spray for pests. This is also when you need to prepare seed trays. While the outside weather may be warming up, try to avoid exposing the plants to fluctuations in temperature and keep things around 42 to 60 degrees. All frost-sensitive plants need to be kept covered if you are struggling to keep the greenhouse temperature above 42.

You can start to sow more plants this month to get a good head start before spring. You should sow bedding plant seeds. You can bring your stored dahlia, hydrangea, and fuchsia into the sunlight. Sow your tomato seeds, as well as eggplants, peas, broad beans, cabbage, sprouts, parsnips, and onions. You can now place strawberry runners into pots.

- **MARCH**

During this time, you need to make sure that the temperature stays between 45 and 65. This may be a good growing time, and when things get up and running, it can also present issues with fluctuating temperatures, depending on the area where you live. These fluctuations can cause problems, as a bright sunny day could cause your greenhouse to become overheated. Aim to keep the temperature around 45 to 65 degrees. Keep the greenhouse heated at night and ventilated during the day. For your young plants, use liquid fertilizer. This is when pests become a bigger issue. If it would help your plants, you can use capillary matting. This is also when you should prepare hanging baskets.

Your bedding plant seedlings from last month should be planted, and you can sow plants that you want to grow in the year right now. Seedlings need plenty of suns, but you will want to protect them from the hottest midday sun as they could easily be scorched. If you wish to, take cuttings from fuchsia and chrysanthemum. Prick out your tomato seedlings, and sow cucumber seeds. You will also need to do some hand pollinating as pollinating insects are not yet active.

- **APRIL**

Hopefully, this month will bring about warmer weather. Make sure the temperature of the greenhouse stays between 45 and 70. Open up the roof vents. On sunny days, use shading or newspaper to cover your seedlings. As always, keep an eye out for pests feeding on your growing plants. You can start using less heat at this time and getting rid of some insulation. Since it is getting warmer, your plants will get thirstier, and you will likely need to water them more often.

This is a good time to sow marigold seeds. Prick out any bedding plants that you're started last month and harden them off. Plant your dahlia cuttings, along with sweet peas and pansies. Prick out the side shoots. Move the cucumbers into a bigger, growing space. Sow zucchini and marrow for May or June plant outs. You can start to harvest some strawberries. You can split and re-pot certain houseplants.

- **MAY**

You will likely have a greenhouse full of vibrant, healthy plants this month, so you get to look forward to spending some extra time in there to stay on top of ventilation and watering. This also means you are moving away from keeping the greenhouse warm to keep the greenhouse cool.

When sunny, make sure the greenhouse temperature stays below 80. You can use shading, especially along with the south-facing glass. You may still need some heating during the night. Open your ventilators if you have to, and open the door as well if need be.

Plants are actively growing at this time, and tying and staking may need to be performed during this time. If you are not growing plants directly in the ground, you have to regularly feed them because the plant's roots can seek out food from the earth. If you are looking to stimulate the leaves' growth, you will need high-nitrogen feed and high-potassium feed when they are flowering or producing fruit.

- **JUNE**

You should no longer need greenhouse heating. Service and store the heaters until the winter. Scorching is a bigger problem at this point. Some common scorching signs are growth slowing down, flowers lacking color, and leaves showing scorch signs. Continue to use shading on plants that are prone to scorching. Keep the temperature down in the greenhouse by ventilating. Water and feed your plants regularly. Damp down the floors during sunny to cool weather and humidity. If you are keeping any outside garden type, you can move those plants out of the greenhouse and harden them off for planting. Clean and tidy up your trays and pots.

- **JULY**

As summer gets closer to its peak, the main problem in a greenhouse is making sure it doesn't get too hot. Ventilation is vital to ensure good air circulation. If the temperature is extremely hot, opening all of the vents and propping open the door may not be enough to keep things comfortable inside. You will likely need to use shades and damp down the greenhouse. These will help, but you may need to bring in an air circulating fan to force ventilation and ensure that the temperatures stay in the right range. Continue to use shading on plants prone to scorching.

The higher temperatures also mean your plants will dry out quicker, so water and regularly feed your plants. Continue to damp down the floors and humidify the greenhouse. You can also take cuttings.

- **AUGUST**

Keep an eye out for mold and use a fungicide if you need to be. If grey mold affects any flowers, fruit, or leaves, destroy the affected areas and spray with a fungicide. Regulate your heat with ventilators. Water and feed regularly. You can plant certain bulbs and take cuttings. This is when you should plant cyclamen, narcissus, and hyacinths for Christmas cuttings. You can take cuttings from pelargonium and fuchsia, as well as lavender and hebe cuttings. Continue to harvest peppers, radishes, cucumbers. Plant potatoes in pots for winter harvesting.

With salad crops and flowers at their peak, August is the best time to take stock and reflect on the season's successes so far. Learn from any mistakes you may have made when it comes to creating your plans for the year. You can also store some seeds to use year.

- **SEPTEMBER**

Temperatures will often fluctuate at this time, and heaters might be needed. Get rid of shading for maximum lighting in the greenhouse. Move frost-sensitive plants inside of the greenhouse. Check your plants for pests before you take them into the greenhouse.

Make sure all of your potted plants are brought in before the first frost. Sow sweet peas and pansies for the spring. Store fuchsia and pelargonium plants. Continue to harvest eggplants, peppers. You should clean up your cucumber plants as they should no longer be producing.

- **OCTOBER**

Make sure you keep the greenhouse above 45. Ventilate only on warm days. Water plants carefully and sparingly. Get rid of deadheads, fallen leaves, and so on to prevent mold. Take all of your half-hardy plants inside. Insulate your greenhouse if you need to.

Plant snowdrop, crocus, hyacinth, and tulip bulbs for the spring. Move the chrysanthemums into the greenhouse and cut flowers. Remove the tomato plants once they are finished producing. You can also sow spring cropping s.

- **NOVEMBER AND DECEMBER**

You should think about removing shading and cleaning the glass, framework, and staging with garden-safe disinfectant during this time. This is also the best time to go through and repair any cracks or holes that could cause you to lose heating. During this, you should insulate the greenhouse and make sure any downpipes or gutters aren't blocked with leaves. Ensure that the greenhouse is cool and dry, and ventilated on sunny days. Your heaters will need to be working properly. Also, go through and clean and tidy your flower pots, trays, and so on, and store them neatly so that they are ready for spring.

Chapter - 19

HOW TO START SEEDLINGS SUCCESSFULLY IN YOUR GREENHOUSE AND GROW THEM INTO HEALTHY PLANTS

Once you've chosen your plants, you'll need to get them installed into your raised beds. There are some basic tools you'll need for planting and everyday maintenance techniques and want to have on hand. These include:

- Trowel, hand rake, and weeding fork
- Bulb digger
- Short-handled pitchfork
- Garden hoe or garden ax
- Sturdy gloves
- weeding bucket
- Harvest basket
- Utility scissor/knife and twine
- Hand pruners
- Watering can or hose
- Stakes or trellises for unruly plants
- Tool storage shed or trunk
- A garden journal or journaling software application

Having the proper tools on hand will make any gardening task easier. If you're on a budget, check around at rummage sales and online in your local buy/sell/trade groups for bargains on second-hand tools. You can also take advantage of end-of-season clearance sales at garden centers and home improvement stores. You should use your journal from the beginning to the end of the season to mark down what you're planting, what products you've applied (fertilizer, compost, pesticides, etc.), how much you harvest, and other notes that will help you with dissecting and assessing the season and planning for a year.

PLANTING YOUR SEEDLINGS

When it's time to get your plants installed in your raised beds, you want to make sure you arrange them in a way that will be the most beneficial. If you are installing any perennials, you should choose their location first, and build around them. You want to make sure you aren't placing your heavy feeders, like the nightshades, on each other. Split them up with herbs, legumes, and your flowers, and cucurbits. This will help naturally with pest control and discourage your soil from becoming stripped of its nutrient load.

To physically plant your seedlings, you'll want to make a deeper and wider hole than the pot or seedling cell they are currently in. For small plants, you can use a bulb digger to make even holes. Be sure to use the spacing instructions on the plant tag, so your seedlings have room to spread, grow, and have adequate airflow. You should give the pots or cells a squeeze to loosen up the soil and then grasp the seedling at the stem's base and give it a good wiggle to release it from the pot.

Once the plants are free, gently massage the soil and roots to loosen them up and place them in your holes. Fill in the holes and lightly tamp down the soil around the base of the plant. When all your plants are installed, give the bed a good watering and leave the plants to settle into their new homes. Don't fiddle with them unless they look seriously askew; they will need a few days for their roots to reach out and establish themselves in their new soil. Place the plant tags in the garden to remind you which plants or use a permanent marker and plastic spoons or knives to make your plant markers.

WATERING FOR MAXIMUM PLANT HEALTH

One of the most important functions of a gardener is to provide water for their plants. You have taken responsibility for growing plants where none were growing before, and you must give them the necessities to thrive. I might go so far as to say that watering properly can be the make-or-break key to any garden. Cultivated plants require approximately four inches of water a week to maintain health and promote growth. You need to be able to meet those needs to be successful.

You should plan on watering your garden every day, except if you have had or anticipate heavy rain. Many people choose to water by hand with a hose or watering can, but raised bed gardens are the perfect set-up for adding drip irrigation or a soaker hose system. If your hose spigot is close to your garden, these can be a relatively inexpensive way to make sure you are watering enough, and they are simple to set up.

Soaker hoses and drip irrigation work by delivering water directly to your soil and your plants' roots. Soaker hoses are the more 'primitive' of the technology. These are hoses, capped on the far end, made of absorbent material that you split and run from your fixture, through your beds, and cover with a light coating of soil. When the faucet is opening, water flows through the hose's permeable sides and into your garden. A simple timer added to your spigot can make a world of difference in having well-watered, happy plants. A drip irrigation system is similar but more targeted. Instead of being a porous hose, there are tubes or hoses with holes that can be placed directly near your plants' base. Both systems are available in DIY kits.

—A simple DIY soaker hose system can ensure your garden is adequately watered—

If you are watering with a hose or can, always water the roots, not the leaves. You don't want your plants to get sunscald or invite pathogens to move in on wet foliage. No matter how you choose to water, a rain gauge is a good addition to any garden. They come in a ton of designs from industrial to whimsical, and they help show gardeners of all abilities how much natural moisture your garden is receiving. You'll be surprised. Sometimes the hardest downpours don't shed as much volume as a light rain that lasts hours.

FERTILIZER AND COMPOST FOR OPTIMUM GROWTH

Gardening in raised beds poses a unique challenge in soil health. While you may not have needed to do an initial soil test based on your supplier, you will need to do a little work to keep that soil healthy throughout your first year and beyond because you don't want to have the expense of replacing the soil frequently. You can accomplish healthy soil year after year by liberal use of compost and discerning use of fertilizers.

You cannot ever add too much organic material to your soil, and compost is a fantastic way to achieve this. Whether you make your own or purchase bagged or bulk compost, you can add a layer to your beds at any time, and it will never be too much. Compost is made up of decomposed plant matter and food scraps which is chock full of beneficial microorganisms. It helps create a thriving soil ecosystem in your garden. When you have more healthy organisms in your soil, your garden will retain more moisture and have better soil pore space, allowing for air and water movement to the roots and letting the roots spread for sturdier plants.

—Understanding the life cycle of your vegetables will 1help you know if you need fertilizer—

Fertilizer is a great tool for encouraging continued growth in heavy feeders and alleviating the drain of nutrients for your soil. However, fertilizer isn't a panacea and should be used sparingly and correctly. Too much of it will cause toxicity of nitrogen, phosphorus, and potassium (the big three nutrients). Too much phosphorus running off from your garden into the water table can contribute to larger environmental concerns.

When you use fertilizer partly through the growing system to supplement your garden's nutrition, it is called 'side-dressing.' Be sure to follow all directions on your fertilizer package closely. If your product needs to be diluted, be sure to do so in the proper amount of water. Spray (or sprinkle) only near the roots of the plants you want to fertilize because you don't want to encourage weed growth, either.

Chapter - 20
GROWING FRUITS, HERBS, AND VEGETABLES

Before we begin looking at how to grow plants in your garden, here is an important note: I will be using the term annuals and perennials from here on out, so it might be the right time to introduce you to these terms.

Annuals are plants and crops that have a life cycle lasting for a year. They grow and produce seeds before dying in one season. This is why you have to replace annuals after each season.

Perennials are plants that produce yields from one year to the other. They live for more than two years. You do not have to replace perennials each year. However, if you would like to introduce new perennials, then you may remove the plant.

Now that you are aware of the differences, it is time to add a little sweetness to your garden. What do I mean? We are going, beginning with fruits.

Here are a few notes:

- Growing fruits in your garden take time. They also require more care than other plants and crops you plan to introduce to your garden. You have fruit species like individual berries and grapes that produce their sweet and juicy yield within a few months. The majority of fruits, however, require patience and attention.
- When gardeners mention the word 'fruit,' they usually group three types of plants; fruits, nuts, and berries. The main reason for this is that there are not many differences in how each plant is grown. Hence, for the sake of making explanations easier, I will use the term fruit broadly to denote fruits, nuts, and berries.

Let us dive into an interesting fact, as well. You see, the fruit is any structure that can bear seeds. This is why what you might typically consider a vegetable is a fruit. We had already seen that the tomato is an example

of fruit. But did you know that even cucumbers and peppers are fruits as well?

Just a little fruit for thought in case you were planning to grow cucumbers as vegetables.

FRUITS

When you decide to grow fruit, the most crucial factor you should consider is choosing the right type of fruit for your garden. This choice is all it takes to ensure that you can grow the fruit well. I can understand the feeling of developing a specific type of fruit (which would typically be your favorite). However, before you decide that, try and perform a little research ahead of time.

Here is something you should know about fruit (though I have a feeling some of you may already know this). Fruits do not appear immediately in a plant's life cycle. The flowers begin to boom first (which is a beautiful sight). Then, the petals of the flower begin to strip away. During this process, you will notice the fruit slowly swelling.

Some kinds of fruits are not suitable for growing in a garden. For example, dates are tough to grow and take more attention and work than other types of fruits. But that does not mean you are deprived of choice. Let me introduce you to the usual suspects.

You can successfully grow the following fruits in your garden:

Avocado, plum, cherry, apricot, apple, pear, banana, plum, kumquat, loquat, guava, pineapple, fig, nectarine, crabapple, pomegranate, persimmon, strawberry, blackberry, blueberry, raspberry, kiwi, any citrus fruits, gooseberry, and grapes

Some of the fruits mentioned above are annuals, while others are perennials. This means that each fruit requires different times before they show their yield. You might consider this factor to choose if you want a plant that has a faster result or you are comfortable waiting.

Each fruit grows well in a particular climate. Pick your fruit based on that factor so that you are ready to provide the essential nutrients and developing conditions for the fruit. For example, if it is winter in your region and you would like to grow avocados, you must know that avocados do not grow well in cold seasons. This means that you might have to pick another flower before you enter the right season for avocados.

If you want to know what fruits are ideal for your particular climate, then you can take inspiration from the local stores and farms. What fruits are not in demand? What are the farmers producing in abundance? Which fruit can you easily find in the local supermarket?

HERBS

Look at the official definition for an herb. It might mention that an herb is any plant that has leaves, flowers, or seeds used for various purposes, including flavoring, medicine, and perfume, or as ornamentals. However, what plants are herbs and which are not is sometimes too confusing to wrap your head around. Regardless, let us look at how we can grow these unique plants and add some spice to your garden!

PLANTING HERBS

The things you might notice about herbs is that there are no rules to follow with these plants. They can adapt to different conditions! It makes your job easier, doesn't it?

However, you do need to focus on the type of herb you are growing. Does it require time to increase, or can it proliferate?

TIMING

The thing about most herbs is that they cannot tolerate the cold. Ideally, you need to plant them just after the worst of the cold-temperatures have left the region. This way, you can let them utilize all the benefits of summer (sunlight and warm air in particular) before you get them ready for the winter.

Do not plant them in the heat of summer. They are not mature to handle the heat, which might cause them stress. If you would like to use herbs during winter, you could consider growing them in containers like pots and keeping them inside the greenhouse.

You could also use the below tips when planting herbs:

- Herbs require the same growing conditions as vegetables. There is no need to focus on just one type of plant when you can simultaneously grow multiple plants. This way, you can even manage to get your vegetables and herbs at the same time if everything goes well! Perfect for some delicious comfort food!
- Combining them with flowers is also another good idea. You can use the flowers when they are in bloom and, at the same time, get your herbs as well. Additionally, you could even use the herbs in your flower arrangement. That sort of structure helps you create a beautiful display.
- Alternatively, you can create an herb garden. This is not just beautiful but also helps you focus on your herbs entirely. For many people, they prefer to use their gardens just for herbs. This allows them to buy their vegetables but use the herbs from their garden.

PLANTING YOUR HERBS

Unlike fruits, you might need to take special care when planting your herbs. Here are some tips for you to follow:

- Get your trowel ready. Find a nice spot that is covered by sufficient sunlight. Ideally, make sure you have well-drained soil. Once you find the place, dig a hole into it. The size of the hole should be slightly more significant than the pot carrying the herb. Add compost and organic fertilizer. Seek out local professionals' help to let you know which one you should use for the purpose.

- Now remove the plant from the pot. Remember never to pull the plant by its leaves. You have to get the plant intact, not with its leaves missing. If that happens, you don't have a plant anymore. You just have a stem!

- Now examine the stem of the plant. Look for a soil line. This is a line that shows where the soil ends and where you can see the stem.

VEGETABLES

- Now we get to the good part - vegetables! There are so many to choose from. To get your vegetables in order, you must begin with the planning phase.

LOCATION

- Find a place in your garden where you would like to start. Make sure that you know what vegetable or vegetables you intend to plant. With a smaller space, you always have room to expand based on future decisions. For example, you might choose to add a different vegetable to the one you are growing right now.

- More people underestimate the value of having a visual depiction of the entire plan. You are essentially doing this to ensure that you do not give away too much space to one vegetable.

- When you are working with vegetables, do not leave empty spaces. When you are done with one crop, utilize that space to grow the vegetable ideal for the coming season. For example, if you had just harvested a summer vegetable, then you should use the space available for a winter vegetable. However, this method is a little tricky, so expect some disappointments before you master the technique.

MORE SUNLIGHT

- When you are growing vegetables, you need to make sure that you are working with the sun. There should not be obstacles nearby that block out sunlight. The sun helps the plant directly and warms up the soil, keeping both plant and soil healthy. However, some vegetables require less sun. In such cases, you have to use a covering material such as a mesh or blind.

PLANTING METHODS

- You might be using the ground to plant your vegetables or make use of a raised bed. You should approach both these surfaces differently when you are working with vegetables.

NATURAL GROUND

- When working on natural ground, make sure that the vegetables' roots have sufficient space to grow. You might encounter sod, which is virtually grass and the soil that it holds. You can remove this layer effectively by using a spade.
- If you encounter weeds, then make sure you have the right tools to get rid of them. You can always make use of a weeder to rip out stubborn weeds.

RAISED BEDS

- With raised beds, you avoid all the work you put into the ground. You already have good drainage inside a raised bed, and if you encounter weeds, you can remove them quickly. Like using a natural environment, make sure that you provide enough depth for the vegetables' roots, depending on the vegetable, of course. Use high-quality soil to fill up the raised bed. This is necessary because you might encounter fewer problems as you work with your vegetables.

SOIL TACTICS

- Whether you prefer to use a natural bed or a raised bed, you need to make sure that the soil is in good condition for the plant.

Chapter - 21
HOW TO GROW PLANTS

Did you know that in a greenhouse, you could succeed in growing all kinds of fruit? Most gardeners know that in a greenhouse, they can grow strawberries but did you know that melons, grapes, peaches, nectarines, and citrus fruits were also successfully grown?

In a greenhouse environment, several varieties of grapes can be grown, including Black Hamburgh and Buckland Sweetwater. In cooler conditions, they are ideal grapes to produce. Gardeners need to pay special attention to open, free-drying soil for the vines and prevent waterlogged soil. When they first become known, they will need to help young plants. In the following winter, the side-shoots produced in the summer will have to be pruned by cutting them back (spur pruning) to their last seed. For good quality grapes, a good quality fertilizer and ample water that reaches all the roots are important.

In both the cool greenhouse and the heated greenhouse, peaches and nectarines can be successfully grown. The nectarine varieties of Humboldt and Pine Apple fit the cold greenhouse. In a greenhouse as well as the Hale's early variety, the Peregrine grows great as long as there is another variety nearby for pollination.

Peaches and nectarines grown in a greenhouse tend to have compact root systems, so they will need to be watered frequently and fed once the tree is established during their growing season. Using a small fine brush, you'll need to transfer pollen from flower to flower. During the flowering period, you will need to do this manual pollination every day. During the flowering season, the greenhouse humidity should be increased. If the fruits are about the walnuts' size, you may need to dilute them to about two fruits per branch foot.

In the greenhouse environment, citrus fruits such as oranges and tangerines can all be successfully grown.

It is challenging to grow any kind of fruit in the greenhouse, as conditions must be right, and pests and disease can be problems that need to be conquered, but it can be done.

Greenhouses give gardening enthusiasts the ability to grow their favorite plants throughout the year. Although it is often a common misconception that flowers and fruit cannot be grown in the same environment, a greenhouse environment where both flowers and fruit can thrive can be created through proper planning.

Growing flowers and fruit can be as simple as designating a set of flower benches and another set of fruit trees or as complex as creating independent greenhouse zones. To avoid potential problems, the identification of greenhouse zones will take place during the greenhouse planning phase. Zones are greenhouse areas that have their unique temperature and climate; they are created by using indoor walls to shape greenhouse s. An automatic control system can maintain different temperatures and humidity levels.

The use of growing lights will enable both flower and fruiting plants to spread. For example, when grown under a rising sun, strawberries thrive; just be sure to use the ever-bearing strand as strawberries from "June Bearing" do not grow indoors. High-pressure sodium (HPS) growing lights are ideal for both fruit and flowering plants, providing a high-efficiency yellow glow with a life expectancy of about 5 years or 24,000 hours.

Every plant has its own growing needs; some key factors to consider in your greenhouse when growing flowers and fruit include: lighting, humidity, and temperature. Plant lighting requirements may vary from full sunlight to heavily shaded environments. Many fruits need direct sunlight to grow, such as strawberries, while flowers do well in shaded areas, such as begonias.

Throughout the year, the amount of humidity needed by plants will differ significantly. Growing calla lilies and in the same area may seem like a good idea at first glance because both need a similar humidity range of 80 to 90 percent, but a second look reveals that need a lower humidity level (65 to 75 percent) at night to grow. The temperature range should also be considered. Most fruits will grow best in the warmer temperature ranges, while flowers can thrive at cooler temperatures.

Through proper planning, flowers and fruit can be successfully grown together, including ranges of lighting, humidity, and temperature. For more detail about the rise of flowers and fruits in your greenhouse, contact a greenhouse expert.

Chapter - 22
GREEN HOUSE TO GROW VEGETABLES AND FRUITS ALL YEAR ROUND

Market greenhouse workers attempt to plan their planting so they can offer clients a constant inventory of new blossoms, herbs, and vegetables all through the developing season. This distribution assists cultivators with arranging planting times and progression planting.

The best way to deal with getting ready for a ceaseless collection is to keep acceptable creation records from past developing seasons and contrast notes and other neighborhood cultivators. You likewise can discover information in seed indexes and extension announcements.

You have to know or have the option to gauge:

- Appropriate planting dates
- Number of days to gather
- Length of gather from first to last pickings

These elements are influenced by a few things. Climate, for instance, is a significant variable. Suitable planting dates are ordinarily around the standard yearly ice-free period in the spring and the usual annual first-freeze time in the fall. You can get these dates for your territory from your nearby Extension specialist or greenhouse store.

Climate affects timing as a result of its impact on seedling buildup crop development. For instance, peas planted at the first conceivable planting date in the spring and afterward again two weeks after the fact will typically develop just a single week separated. Germination conditions at the time planting will probably be significantly improved, and the young plants will become quicker as the days stretch, gradually finding the primary crop. This equivalent procedure occurs backward for fall crops. Indeed, even a few days' distinctions in midsummer planting dates can lead to a collect date distinction of two, or even three, weeks.

Two different ways to broaden the collect time frame for specific crops are 1) to plant assortments with an alternate number of days to development simultaneously, and 2) to plant a similar assortment on various occasions in progression.

Sweet corn frequently is developed in successive plantings to draw out the gathering season. A decent method to amaze sweet corn plantings is to hold up until one harvest. Sweet corn will grow in general rise all the more gradually in cool soil (50–55°F) than in heat soil (68–77°F). Standard sweet corn assortments are preferable for late-winter plantings over the super-sweet assortments since the super-sweet assortments won't also proceed in cool soil. Planting sweet corn around a multi-week before the asserted age ice-free date is a general guideline for the earliest plantings. On the last part of the planting season, make your last planting around 80 days before the usual first fall ice date. Notwithstanding successive plantings, you can plant assortments that require various time allotments to arrive at development. For instance, some sweet corn assortments are reproduced to develop in 70 days, while others require 100 days.

Planting as per ideal soil temperature is another usual method to prpare plantings. The table underneath, Soil temperature Germination Ranges for Select Vegetables, gives a quick synopsis.

Soil Temperature Germination Ranges for Select Vegetables	
TEMP (° F)	***PLANT***
45–85	Cabbage, kale, broccoli, collards (germinate well at 85, seedlings prefer 45–65)
35–80	And most salad greens (at more than 80, the germination rate drops 50%)
35–75	Spinach (optimum 68)
50–85	Onions (optimum 75)
45–95	Radishes (optimum 85)
50–85	Beets, (optimum 85)
60–85	Beans snap and dry (optimum 80)
70–85	Beans, lima (optimum 85)
40–75	Peas (optimum 75)
60–95	Corn (optimum 95)
65–82	(Optimum 80)
60–95	Peppers (optimum 85)
65–100	Cucumbers, melons, squash (optimum 80–95)

Bugs and infections are another primary consideration that can influence creation scheduling. In the muggy southeast, tomato developers regularly plant both spring and fall tomato crops on the grounds that the early plants surrender to infection in mid-summer. A market plant specialist in North Carolina reports that she sets out multiple times during the developing season. She likewise noticed that squash vine borer is so awful in summer squash that she just gets around about fourteen days of reap from each planting.

SUCCESSION PLANTING

When you have a design of conceivable individual arrangements for successive plantings, the Succession Planting graph on the following page can be utilized as a layout and adjusted for your area.

CROP	seed to flat, planned	seed to flat, actual	plant to the field, planned	plant to the field, actual	Estimated days to harvest	actual days to harvest	length of harvest	interval between plantings	comments
Arugula					30			2 weeks	Best in cool weather
Beans, bush					60			2 weeks	Summer
Beans, lima					65			*	Summer
Beans, pole					60-70			*	Summer
Beets					40-70			2 weeks	Spring & fall
Broccoli					60-70 f.t.			2 weeks	Spring & fall
Cabbage					70-80 f.t.			3 weeks	Spring & fall
Carrots					85-95			3 weeks	Spring & fall
Cauliflower					50-65 f.t.			2 weeks	Spring & fall

Collards					60-100			*	Fall
Corn, sweet					70-100			2 weeks	Summer
Cucumbers					60			4-5 weeks	Summer
Edamame					70			*	Summer
Eggplants					65 f.t.			8 weeks	Summer
Kale					40-50			2 weeks	Spring & fall
Kohlrabi					50-60			2 weeks	Spring & fall
Head					70-85			2 weeks	Spring & fall
Leaf					40-50			2 weeks	Best in cool weather
Muskmelons					80-90			2 weeks	Summer
Okra					70			*	Summer
Onions, dry					90-120 f.t.			*	
Onions, green					85			2-3 weeks	
Greens					30-60			2 weeks	Best in cool weather
Peas					55-70			*	Spring & fall
Peas, southern					65			*	Summer
Peppers					60-70 f.t.			*	Summer
Potatoes					90			*	Spring & fall
Pumpkins					90-120			*	Summer
Radishes					25-30			2 weeks	Best in cool weather

Radishes, daikon					60-75			*	Spring & fall
Spinach					50-60			2 weeks	Spring & fall
Squash, summer					45-60			4-8 weeks	Summer
Squash, winter					90-120			*	Summer
					65-90 f.t.			2	Summer
					35-40			2 weeks	Best in cool weather

Chapter - 23
HOW TO GROW FLOWERING PLANTS

At times, it can be nice to break up the growth of fruits, vegetables, and herbs with a bright and sunny flower. Your greenhouse garden doesn't have to house only food for consumption—you can grow flowers too! There is a wide array of flowers that you can grow in your greenhouse simply for fun, or have a fresh supply of flowers for the vase on your dining room table.

There are also practical reasons to grow flowers. Edible flowers do exist, and they can add a spot of color to an otherwise boring-looking dish. I want to give you a few hints and tips on growing your own flowers — edible and not so edible.

EDIBLE FLOWERS

No matter what type of mood you are in, flowers can always brighten a less than a subpar day. This can also be said for edible flowers! They can take a plain dinner plate into a beautiful-looking medley of food. A bolt of color is all you need to bring a smile to your face during dinner. Fortunately for us, we can grow some flowers to eat! A few common edible flowers are:

- Daylilies
- Calendulas
- Carnations
- Begonias
- Pansies
- Violets

Let's take a look at what it takes to grow some of these edible flowers, as well as some tidbits of information

on them.

CALENDULA

An annual flower that often brings a smile to the face of anyone who sees the bright colors that bestow the petals of this flower. Similar to sunflowers, the calendula will turn to face the sunlight during the day.

They are marked by bright oranges and yellows that grace the petals. This flower tastes a little like pepper and has a great bite to it.

It is popular in the world of edible flowers because of its great taste, its bright colors, and the fact that it is easy to grow.

Keep in mind when cultivating this flower that it is the petals that are edible. Don't try and eat any other parts of the flower. You can dry the petals and use them to infuse teas, add peppery notes into creams, and simply add in a bright spot on a dark dish. The most common food recipes you will find calendula will be in salads and soups that are made from cream. Sometimes it comes as merely a garnish.

There are medicinal benefits to the calendula flower as well. It is known to reduce both acne breakouts and inflammation.

Their most common enemy is the aphid; however, if your greenhouse is clean and the air fresh, you will lessen the risk of being visited by this garden pest.

Once you start the seed, you will wait around 14 days for germination to occur. They like sunny and warm weather, so regular climate conditions in your greenhouse should be perfect to house the beautiful flowers. If you start them in the spring, then you will most likely have them bloom in fall. They are considered a late annual flower.

Side note: it is advised that if you are pregnant or trying to get pregnant, you avoid eating calendula flowers to affect your reproductive system.

DAY LILIES

This beautiful perennial flower is a delectable and edible part of the cuisine. You can eat every part of the lily from the stem to the petals and even the roots every day! One of the most common types of cuisine where you see daylilies used is in Chinese food.

The flower itself has a mild taste which is a mixture of root vegetables and sweet watermelon. The sweetest part of the flower will be the buds and flower petals. You can consume them raw or cook them in your meals. These are also commonly used to brighten up desserts and bring a flair of color to dishes. The roots can taste

like potatoes when they are steamed or boiled and provide a unique dish. The leaves on its stem can also be eaten. These can add a unique spin to your green garden salad.

My recommendation to the beginner grower is to go to your local nursery and buy a starter plant. The day lily plant can take up to two years to blossom when it is first planted from seed.

Thankfully these are hardy flowers, and they last in various types of climates. For planting daylilies, ensure their containers have good drainage systems. You can also plant them in greenhouse beds, simply ensure that each seedling is planted about 18 inches apart from each other. Your day lilies will need to be watered every day. As the flowers die, you should deadhead them (remove the dead flower head from the stalk) so that they can re-grow. If you start in smaller containers, you can transplant them as long as the sapling is about 4 inches tall. If you are transplanting them into greenhouse beds, you should wait to reach 5 to 6 inches.

If you've never seen the flower decorate your plate at dinner, then you've definitely seen them at parks or even in your garden.

However, you might not have known that this popular garden flower is also edible! They taste great in salads, even desserts, and some fancy drinks. They often accompany dinner plates as a garnish because of their bright colors.

These flowers enjoy lots of shade and moist soil. They still need sunlight; however, they do need to be protected by the harsh sunlight from the mid-afternoon. They love a lot of moisture, so you should water them daily. Make sure that the soil is moist and not water-logged. A key sign that you are not watering your plants enough is if their leaves have started to wilt and fall off.

INEDIBLE FLOWERS

Greenhouses are common homes for flowers because their climatic conditions can be so controlled to extend the growing period and save flowers from frosty weather. There are quite a few flowers that rank high on the list of favorites for a greenhouse. They are:

- Amazon Lilies
- Chenille Plants
- African Violets
- Chinese Hibiscus

It goes without saying those are some of the most popular flowers chosen to be cultivated inside a greenhouse. The reason for this is because they are such sensitive plants that a weather too cold or too warm will have an adverse effect on their growth.

There is a large variety in existence today. Each with their own set of care instructions. You need to decide which type of orchid you want to grow and the specific conditions that are required to nurture it to its best-blooming potential.

Contrary to popular belief, most end up dying due to overwatering rather than underwatering. Your orchid needs water, but be careful because overwatering will lead to root rot. My best advice to you is to wait for your orchid to dry out before you water it again.

Possibly one of the most iconic flowers, also the most romantic to hand to a loved one as a thoughtful gesture, reign over the most popular flowers in general. Whether you're a gardener who gardens as a hobby, provider for the family, and even on a larger scale. often, people try their hands to cultivate a flower.

The first step towards growing in a greenhouse is to wisely choose the kind of rose you plan to grow. It's important to keep in mind the climate of your greenhouse when picking this will give you your biggest chance of success when it comes to growing these beautiful blooms.

The great benefit of cultivating inside a greenhouse is that you lessen the risk of pests and other diseases, and fungal infections. If you choose to plant a rose tree that is specifically designed to be resistant to pests, then that will work in your greenhouse too.

You can plant from seeds, but I highly recommend that you buy a starter plant from your local nursery. If

you use a starter plant, you will want to transplant it into a new container when you bring it home. Your container should be roughly 9 inches in diameter. If you fill smaller rocks at the bottom of your container, you create better drainage for your plant, and it is a step in the prevention of root rot.

The potted need to be in a space where they can get some sunlight (or even artificial light). They need roughly 6 hours of light every single day in order to blossom at their full potential. You need to space out your rose pots so that they don't overshadow each other as they grow. Roughly six feet of distance between rose pots is a good idea.

As your rose plants grow, you will need to prune the bushes so that the branches stay around 3-4 inches from the stem. This means all of your budding blooms as well. The fewer stems and leaves your bush has, the bigger the flowers it will produce for you.

If you notice dead branches (the telltale sign is that the branch will be brown on the inside), you need to trim them away and keep them away from blocking the plant. Your main goal is to promote air circulation so that moisture doesn't build up between the leaves of your rose bush.

The soil in the pots of your needs to be moist but not water-logged (you're probably tired of hearing this but for a novice gardener it really needs to be drilled into your memory). Depending on the climate in your greenhouse the amount of water you use to water and keep the soil moist can vary from day to day. Water should not touch the stems or leaves of rose bushes-especially buds and branches should be avoided to prevent water from accumulating under the leaves and in the bushes. A fertilizer that is high in phosphorus should be applied to the soil whenever you see new leaves grow and then roughly two weeks from the date of new growth.

Flowers do require active maintenance, and you mustmake sure that they are growing well under your care. As long as you check in on them and monitor them, you should be able to have beautiful blossoms in your greenhouse—not to mention their beautiful aroma alone is enough to keep them around.

Chapter - 24
OVERWINTERING YOUR GREENHOUSE AND EXTENDING YOUR GROWING SEASONS INTO THE COLDER MONTHS

PLANTING IN COLD WEATHER

The main reason why people create greenhouses is because it allows them to plant all year round. To be more specific, they are preparing for the colder months of fall and winter. While having a greenhouse will provide you the opportunity to grow the so-called winter plants effectively, it is no guarantee that you'll be able to raise them well. You'll still need to equip yourself with the right techniques for raising plants in cold weather. There are some tips that can help you get by, as well as some plants that are best suited for such weather conditions.

Growing cold weather plants during the winter seasons allows you to make very minimal adjustments to your greenhouse conditions. Often times, the minimum amount of sunlight received during these cold periods is more than enough to provide heat sufficient enough for these plants to survive. In fact, subjecting them to summer-type temperatures can prove detrimental to their growth. Another advantage of planting cold-weather plants during this season is the fact that they can withstand even occasional freezing temperatures.

There is a huge variety of plants that can be considered at home with cold weather. You can grow these plants in low-temperature, low-light conditions without encountering too many problems. Among the staples of cold weather, growing include leafy plants such as cabbage and spinach. Under these conditions, cruciferous vegetables (such as broccoli and cauliflower) can also flourish. Also, plants that grow massive roots, such as beets and carrots, are known to be cold weather plants. Other plants that are known to thrive during this time of the year include peas, radishes, green onions, chard, and kohlrabi.

A lot of these plants are capable of growing with minimal supervision and without any special treatment. Of course, you must ensure that you always provide adequate care for the plants. To ensure that your plants would grow accordingly, here are some tips that can prove useful.

AVOID EXTREME TEMPERATURES

While cold weather plants are resilient to temperature changes, it is not advisable to expose them to extreme cold or heat. Make sure not to make your greenhouse either too hot or too cold. As these plants are more used to cool weather, too much heat would not be conducive to their growth. As a final reminder, it's not healthy for the plants to be subjected to temperature fluctuations as it's a source of stress for them.

KEEP THE LIGHT FLOWING

Getting light is a bit tricky, especially during the winter season. As days are shorter during the cold months, you'll need to make the most out of the sunlight that comes in. However, you might need to supplement some light through your built-in lighting system. This is especially so for seedlings still at the nursery. In fact, some seeds don't sprout without enough light. As a guide, study the photoperiod of the specific plant you intend to cultivate.

Chapter - 25

UNDERSTAND HOW TO MAINTAIN YOUR SYSTEM AND CARE FOR YOUR PLANTSSEASONS INTO THE COLDER MONTHS

The effort applied in keeping a thing in its proper condition is referred to as maintenance. It refers to actions carried out to a hazard from happening and can also, before starting your greenhouse garden, it is essential to know how to maintain it. It is even arguable that more than knowing how to begin your greenhouse garden, it is much more important to understand how to keep it. This is because the success of the plants you are growing depends on your ability to maintain the greenhouse. Remember that the purpose of creating a greenhouse is to provide a conducive growing environment for your plants and protect them against adverse weather conditions. It is then expected that plants grown in a greenhouse should outperform the ones grown in an open field. The conservatory allows you to successfully cultivate plants that are usually not suitable for your environment. The many benefits a greenhouse garden offers should be enough motivation to maintain it to get the best of it. Keeping your greenhouse may and may not be expensive; greenhouse maintenance costs depend on many factors. The size of your greenhouse and the type of plants being grown are significant determinants; therefore, it is wise to choose a greenhouse whose maintenance is within the available capital. For new growers, maintaining the greenhouse may seem complicated, but it becomes a straightforward thing to do with time and the right understanding.

HOW TO MAINTAIN THE RIGHT TEMPERATURE IN THE GREENHOUSE

Regardless of your greenhouse size, the system temperature is one of the critical factors determining successful cultivation. Below are tips on how to maintain the right greenhouse temperature:

Install sensors or, better yet, a monitoring system in your greenhouse. This will help to monitor the change in the temperature of your greenhouse. Some sensors will also give feedback on the moisture level of your greenhouse.

Ensure sufficient ventilation. The enclosed greenhouse can sometimes create a heated growing environment; adequate ventilation is needed to keep the right temperature range. Install cooling systems such as fans or air conditioners depending on your greenhouse size and plant type.

Pay attention to your lighting in the system. Depending on the external weather condition, adjust your greenhouse lighting accordingly to maintain the right temperature. Install grow lights if necessary, and you may also want to consider installing heaters.

HOW TO MAINTAIN THE RIGHT RELATIVE HUMIDITY IN A GREENHOUSE

The humidity here refers to the amount of moisture in the greenhouse growing environment. It is no news that keeping the wrong humidity in the greenhouse is detrimental to its growth. Here are a few tips on how to maintain the right relative humidity:

Avoid overwatering your growing medium. Too much watering is the beginning of trouble in the plants' root system. The humidity level in the greenhouse increases when there is too much water in the medium.

Ensure enough air circulation. This will improve the ventilation in the greenhouse and invariably ensure the right humidity level.

MAINTAINING YOUR GREENHOUSE IN COLD WEATHER

Keeping the greenhouse in the right condition can be extreme in cold weather, especially during the winter season. However, the following tips can help to maintain your greenhouse during this period easily:

Use a thermostat to monitor your greenhouse temperature level to know how much heat you need to supply.

Install a heater in your greenhouse. This is very helpful in an extremely cold climate. Heat up your greenhouse environment to the needed degree to keep your plants healthy but keep in mind that even in the cold season, the weather condition changes during daytime and night time. Therefore, install a good and reliable thermometer that will indicate the temperature changes accurately.

Another tip is to ensure that your heater size is sufficient to cover your entire plantation. If your greenhouse is too large for the heater size, you may restrict your greenhouse and heat up the area suitable for the heater size for effectiveness.

With the right temperature, light intensity, and humidity put in place in the greenhouse system, other required maintenance comes down to frequent inspection to ensure a tidy environment, pest-free plants, and any error, quickly making adjustments before it becomes a bigger issue. If all these maintenance guidelines seem a bit too much for you at first, keep at it because it only gets better and easier in greenhouse gardening.

Chapter - 26
LEARN HOW TO UTILIZE LIGHTENING AND IRRIGATE YOUR PLANTS FOR OPTIMAL GROWTH

There's a lot more greenhouse lighting than the eye can see. Growers looking for suitable lighting for their greenhouse should consider the following three factors: the type of crop being cultivated, the time of year, and the amount of sunlight available.

Greenhouses typically allow six hours of direct or full-spectrum light every day. If this cannot be achieved naturally, external lighting must be used. Additional lighting is the use of multiple high-intensity artificial lighting to promote crop growth and yield. Hobbyists use them to maintain growth and extend the growth period, while commercial growers like to use them to increase yields and profits.

Photoperiod control lighting is equally essential as additional lighting. Growers have a wide range of lighting options to choose from, so it is essential to understand different lighting types complexities. Let's look at the uses and advantages of four different types of lighting.

HIGH-PRESSURE SODIUM FIXTURES

High-pressure sodium fixtures provide more orange and redder spectrum light and give the human eye a golden-white appearance. As they promote budding and flowering, they are generally used in the growth cycle of the plant. These fixtures are approximately seven times more effective than incandescent bulbs and work best when used in combination with natural daylight, making them an excellent choice for greenhouses. High-pressure sodium lights also offer the potential for a 10% increase in intensity and photo-synthetically active radiation (PAR). They give high-pressure sodium lights about 4 to 5 minutes to warm up and one minute to cool down. That's why they're not perfect at places where lights turn on and off regularly. It is also essential to be cautious of the placement; high-pressure sodium lights should be placed 30 to 36 inches above the plant for optimal performance.

FIXED AND PROGRAMMABLE SPECTRUM LED FIXTURES

LED (light-emitting diode) fixtures are the longest-lasting choice provided by Growers Supply, with a typical lifespan of 50,000 hours. The LED diode won't flame out as quickly as regular light bulbs, which gives it an extremely long-life cycle. LED light fixtures are more efficient than standard lighting because more of the power input goes to light than to heat. For example, incandescent bulbs are only about 20% effective, as most of their input power is used to generate heat.

Perhaps one of the biggest benefits of LED lighting is significant energy savings. They are quickly incorporated into any project and deliver up to 70% savings compared to high-intensity discharge (HID) lighting.

There is no time required to warm up with an LED fixture, and they are also free of mercury, making disposal much more comfortable than other bulbs. LEDs provide superior functionality when used as the sole source of lighting, making them an attractive option for many growers.

CERAMIC METAL HALIDE

Ceramic metal halide lamps are utilized for their blue light, even though they appear bright white to the human eye. They can easily act as a primary light source, with an estimated lifetime of between 8,000 and 15,000 hours. Because metal halides are 3 to 5 times more effective than incandescent bulbs, they are an excellent choice for areas that do not receive natural sunlight.

It is important to remember that metal halides need to be warmed up for around 5 minutes or less before they can give out maximum light. They do need a cool downtime of around 5 to 10 minutes before restarting. For this reason, they are not suggested for locations where the lights are frequently turned on and off.

Ceramic metal halide lights should be placed 30 to 36 inches above the plants and may darken leaves and the overall good-looking greenery. A Growers Supply PAR Lucent Ceramic Metal Halide Lights are perfect for use in greenhouse and hydroponic applications. Growers also use them in the early stages of plant life while seeds are in the vegetative growth process. The dimmable ballast enables growers to obtain the perfect light for their operation. They're quiet, too, so there's no annoying humming, clicking, or high-pitched noise to contend with.

T5 FIXTURES

T5 fixtures are the most effective and common choice for fluorescent greenhouse lighting. They use more limited energy than traditional lamps and can last up to 50,000 hours. These environmentally friendly lights also feature aluminum reflectors for optimum efficiency. They are best suited for use in hydroponics, greenhouses, farms, barns, and more. They can be used from the beginning of the seed phase to full-term development.

The letter "T" indicates the lamp's tubular shape, and the number 5 denotes the diameter of the lamp in eighths of an inch. T5 lamps are thin, only 5/8 "inch in diameter, making T5 fluorescent tubes more effective than conventional fluorescent tubes.

GrowSpan's High-Performance 45 "T5 Fluorescent Lamp highlights exceptionally high lumen output and full-spectrum lighting that is excellent for plants from the seedling stage to full-term growth. Its minimal heat output suggests that it can be placed very close to plants, within 6 to 12 inches, to be precise. While technically there is nothing as too much light, it is essential not to use too much light in a small space, which can cause the surface area of the leaf to overheat.

With so many greenhouse lighting choices customized to different plant types and growth stages, it's easy to see why expert advice is so respected by growers everywhere. GrowSpan's wide range of lighting solutions, from additional growth to photoperiod control, optimizes rising space an easy, efficient process.

Chapter - 27
GROWING, CHILIES, PEPPER, SQUASHES, CUCUMBERS

HERBS

Among the easiest and arguably some of the most useful plants to cultivate in your garden, herbs are nearly as indispensable to the home cook as salt and pepper. Additionally, herbs can be readily grown in pots, leaving the bulk of your raised bed to other plants (if using a drip irrigation system, pots are fairly easy to integrate with spot watering emitters). It is undeniably satisfying to simply pop outside and scissor off a small handful of herbs to enhance any meal during the growing season. And many herbs will return each year—again, depending on your location—and be some of the first pleasures to be harvested at the start of the spring.

Herbs can be either direct seeded or grown from seed and transplanted into your garden if you like, though herb seeds are typically so tiny that they are difficult to handle. I prefer to procure seedlings from a reliable local source that uses organic methods, with plant seedlings after the last frost.

SQUASH & THE LIKE

Squash, like okra, can be an over-performer in warm climates, though their easygoing presence ensures likely garden success. Again, squash varieties need space to spread out and flourish, so make sure you have adequate room. Direct seed in spring for a late summer abundance. Try zucchini, yellow crook-necked squash, and patty pan varietals that do well in most regions with a summer stretch.

Other pumpkin varieties, such as acorns and walnuts, mature and grow up. Thus they are good for fall harvesting. However, they need more space and time accordingly. Also, eggplant, which is technically a nightshade plant, is similar in its growing capacity and timing to squash.

CHILE AND OTHER PEPPERS

Chile and bell peppers are colorful and tasty additions to your garden. The larger the pepper, the more room it will need, of course; otherwise, most pepper varieties can be planted in spring for a harvest throughout the summer and into early fall. I have had success with typical peppers like jalapenos, serranos, Anaheims, and poblanos. I've also grown padrons, lovely Spanish peppers that can be sautéed in olive oil and eaten whole (the fun is in the surprise: most are sweet and mild, but one or two will pack a spicy punch); shishitos, a Japanese pepper treated similarly to padrons; habaneros, the super spicy brilliant orange pepper; Bolivian rainbow peppers, more of an ornamental plant with its purple, red, and orange bouquets of small peppers; and huge bushes of cayennes, which I use to make pretty ristras (the pepper wreaths you find in the Southwest) for drying. Grinding your own cayenne powder will ruin you for the dusty supermarket stuff forever. Most peppers are easy to grow—IF you have a decently long summer.

CUCUMBERS

Another prolific, vine-y plant, cucumbers thrive in most warm climates. Since they are so prolific, and since their vines tend to grow willy-nilly, I recommend setting up another small bed for them (which can also be used for larger squash varieties and/or melons) or, at the least, cordoning of the garden to limit the vine expansion within the rest of your bed. There are numerous varieties of cucumbers you can grow, from traditional slicing and pickling cucumbers to Asian types that have fewer seeds. I did not bother with cucumbers for a long time—they are cheap and plentiful in the supermarket, albeit grown industrially and most often coated with wax—until I discovered the Armenian cucumber: these pale varietals produce large, long fruit with small seed pods and a clean, crisp taste that reminds you that cucumbers are closely related to melons. They produce so well (and don't turn bitter even when large) that I supplied a local restaurant for a couple of years from my small patch. One decent-sized Armenian cucumber can provide a side dish for a table of six or eight people. Direct seed in the garden in spring in a plot that gets lots of direct sunshine; most cucumber varieties thrive throughout the hot summer into early fall.

These guys are the reason I started gardening in the first place: compare a homegrown tomato to a supermarket tomato, and you will instantly see why. While all produce tastes better coming out of the ground, fresh and organically grown, in particular showcase the glories of home gardening (and the horrors of what industrial agriculture has done to this beloved fruit). There are so many varieties of out there that a type of tomato can be grown in virtually any location. These plants can be directly seeded indoors in late winter/early spring to transplant after the last frost. Typically, I don't risk planting seedlings until after tax day in my Zone 7 area. Caring for seedlings indoors is time-consuming but cost-effective if you plan on growing lots of tomato plants. I like to get my seedlings locally from an organic producer, as I only grow about six or seven plants each season.

Need direct sun and adequate water throughout the growing season. In my garden, start producing in earnest

in July (I usually get lucky with a couple at the end of June) and continue through October, excepting drought years with 100+ degree temperatures. Once seedlings are planted and start thriving, put up a tomato cage around each plant. Give your tomato plants plenty of room to flourish, and check on them regularly once they start growing fast and producing, gently taming the vines through the cage. Tomato vines will always start to look a bit wild at the height of the growing season, so don't worry too much about that, as long as they are healthy. Also, beware of the avian risks from above: the first year I planted tomato seedlings, I left them alone for a couple of hours to make dinner. When I went to check on them that evening, the birds had stripped all the leaves off every single plant! Most survived, but since then, I've strung a makeshift net over the perimeter of the garden—make sure netting is suspended so as not to smother the plants—to prevent such an apocalypse. Just about everyone, birds and bugs and marauding neighborhood children, love.

I like to grow cherry or grape (Black Cherry and Yellow Pear are favorites) in a large pot near the garden, as these smaller plants don't need as much room and often don't require cages. They also mature faster and are ready to pluck off the vine and throw into a salad in mid-summer. For other varieties, I tend to rely on heirloom that is local to my area, such as Arkansas Travelers, Cherokee Purples, and Royal Hillbilly (a rarer heirloom most definitely worth seeking out); check with your local farmers' market or gardening store for what varietals might be common for your location. Other famous heirlooms include Brandywine and Green Zebra (this one remains green when ripe). If you are interested in canning, paste work best for this, the San Marzano being the standard-bearer.

Chapter - 28
UNDERSTANDING THE FERTILIZER LEVEL - PART 2

We have chemicals in our regular lives all over. Shampoo, toothpaste, numerous foods, even our clothing all consist of or are produced with the use of chemicals. Besides contaminating the environment, the usage of chemicals can be much more harmful. But we're focusing on gardening and the utilization of these chemicals in our food.

One of the popular way's chemicals are utilized in food production is via chemical fertilizers. Chemical fertilizers are quick-acting, short-term plant enhancers and account for:

- Degeneration of soil friability, producing hardpan soil
- The devastation of advantageous soil life, including earthworms
- Changing vitamin and protein content of certain crops
- Making certain crops more prone to illness
- Stopping plants from taking in some needed minerals

The soil must be considered as a living entity. A fertilizer, due to its acids, liquefies the cement material, composed of the dead organic of soil organisms, which maintains the rock particles together in the form of ground crumbs. This small surface layer of rock particles urges rainwater to run off instead of entering the soil.

For instance, a highly soluble fertilizer, like 5-10-5, goes into solution in the soil water quickly, so that much of it might be leached away into our groundwater without helping the plants at all. This chemical induces the soil to assume a cement-like hardness.

Numerous artificial chemical fertilizers include acids, sulfuric and hydrochloric, which will enhance the soil's acidity. The alterations accompany alterations on the soil (pH) in the kinds of organisms which can reside in the soil.

There are numerous ways by which artificial fertilizers decrease the soil´s aeration. Earthworms, whose various borings made the soil more permeable, are eliminated. The chemical fertilizers are going to demolish also the cement material, which combines rock hint together in crumbling.

Inorganic fertilizers get plants of some organic immunity by decimating the microorganisms in the soil. Numerous plant illnesses have already been significantly examined when antibiotic-producing bacteria or fungi flourished around the roots. When plants are provided with much nitrogen and just a medium quantity of phosphate, plants will quickly contract infections.

Host resistance is acquired in case there is a small quantity of nitrogen and a large supply of phosphate. Fungus and bacterial illness have been connected to high nitrogen fertilization and the absence of trace elements. Plants cultivated with artificial chemical fertilizers tend to have less nutritional value than organically cultivated plants.

For instance, several tests have discovered that supplying citrus fruits with a large quantity of soluble nitrogen lowers the vitamin C content of oranges. It has also been discovered that these fertilizers that offer soluble nitrogen will reduce the capacity of corn to produce high protein content.

Most likely, the most regularly noted deficiency in plants treated continuously with chemical fertilizers is a shortage of trace minerals. To describe this principle will imply diving into a little bit of physics and chemistry, but you will then quickly see the uneven nutrition created in inorganic fertilized plants.

Every humus particle is negatively charged and will draw in the good elements, like potassium's, sodium's, calcium's, magnesium's, manganese's, aluminum, boron's, irons, coppers, and additional metals. Whenever sodium nitrate is dumped into the soil time after time, a radical shift occurs on the humus particles in large quantities.

So, with chemical fertilizers, in short, you have short-term outcomes and long-term harm to the soil, groundwater, and our health. Another reason to stay clear of the utilization of chemicals and pesticides is that long-term utilization of such chemicals can exhaust the soil and leave it unfit to sustain further growth.

In numerous cases, buds of perennials unexpectedly stop blooming for no obvious reason, and the culprit is frequently found to be the overuse of chemical fertilizers, herbicides, and pesticides.

Chemicals that are administered to plants can frequently seep into the water supply, thus polluting it. While it's correct, our drinking water does go through a filtration procedure; it's been shown that this process doesn't eliminate ALL of the damaging contaminants.

It has also been shown that certain chemicals can cause conditions, congenital disabilities, and other harmful health problems. All one needs to do is see the movie "Erin Brokovich" to see what chemical pollution of

water can do to a body.

Consumers are also worried about toxic sewage utilized as fertilizer on conventional farms. Organic farming forbids the utilization of sewage sludge. They worry about untried and unlabelled genetically created food ingredients in common grocery store items.

Genetically created ingredients are now discovered in 60 percent to 75 percent of all U.S. foods. Even though polls suggest 90 percent of Americans yearn for labels on gene-altered foods that governments and industries don't want to label. Organic production restricts genetic engineering. Eating organic gets rid of, or reduces, the danger of being poisoned by heavy metals discovered in sewage sludge, the unknowns of genetically modified food, the swallowing of hormone residues, and the exposure to mutant bacteria strains.

It likewise decreases the exposure to insecticide and fungicide remains. Residues from possible carcinogenic pesticides are left behind on a few of our beloved vegetables and fruits. In 1998, the FDA found pesticide remains in over 35 percent of the food that was tested. Numerous U.S. products have been tested as being more poisonous than those from other countries. What's worse is that existing standards for pesticides in food do not yet consist of specific defense for fetuses, infants, or young children regardless of major changes to federal pesticide laws in 1996 calling for such reforms.

It is absolutely in the human population's best interests to stay clear of chemicals in our food, but it's also far better for our planet. Chemicals can impact the soil making it less productive. They damage important parts of the natural eco-system. All plants and animals perform some kind of purpose, even if that purpose isn't particularly apparent.

By taking these components out of the natural life cycle, we are jeopardizing our environment in means we can't automatically see outright, but that danger is there. So, it ends up being obvious that cultivating your food naturally is the best way to go. Let's take a second and look at what precisely organic gardening is.

Chapter - 29
DIFFERENT TYPES OF PLANTS YOU CAN GROW DURING THE WARM AND COLD SEASON

COOL SEASON VEGETABLES

Depending on the particular type of garden, a gardener may be interested in cultivating food sources during the colder season. Not all types of vegetable are cultivated during the summer and spring season because there as certain types of vegetables that can thrive very well in colder weather, such as the following:

- Cauliflower
- Onions
- Mustard
- Carrots
- Broccoli
- Spinach
- Kohlrabi
- Turnip

Cultivate these vegetables during both winter and fall and watch them grow. Because colder months yield lower temperatures, it will be unlikely for a gardener to apply any natural pesticides to their vegetables, making them organic and tastier.

Plant these winter vegetables close to a south-facing wall or other windbreaks so that you can take advantage of the higher temperature as well as the protection to extend the growing season by a few weeks.

WARM SEASON VEGETABLES

These can be grown in tubs and pots, which give you easy access to one of the most common edibles in our different home recipes. They usually demand lots of nutrients supply for proper growth and frequent watering with much exposure to sunlight in order to get them well ripened. When growing your vegetables, remember to choose a location with minimum sunlight exposure of 6 hours, although about 8–10 hours of sun is best for them. All varieties are suitable for a container, but the determinate types (compact plants, bush plants, or patio plants) are usually the best plants to grow in containers. They are very reliable and predictable because they set their flowers and fruits all at once, and they typically grow to a predetermined size (about 3–4 ft. in height). The stockier bush and smaller tumbling varieties will not require pruning as they grow. You can plant a few marigolds alongside as this will add color as well as produce a scent that helps to repel aphids. The variety of plants should be relative to the size of the container used as they are very productive. You should also make use of a potting mix made up of some loam to help retain moisture for a longer time.

BEANS

Beans are great and very productive when grown in containers. They are quite easy to grow but also require enough sun and deep pots. The depth of the container usually depends on the plant variety. Bush beans require about 6–7 inches container depth, while pole beans need about 8–9 inches of container depth. You are advised to use unglazed containers with good drainage to allow the evaporation of excess water. Once your bean seeds germinate, which usually takes about 5 or 7 days, remember to conserve soil moisture by spreading mulch lightly over the surface of the soil. Beans require a well-drained soil mix with high organic content for healthy growth. You may have to grow pole beans close to a wall or provide them with long support like a trellis, as they are climbers. It is advisable that if you're growing beans in a very large container, combine summer savory, kale, or celery with them. Inspect them regularly for insects, and don't wait too long before you harvest your beans else they will become tough.

SQUASHES

These plants are best for rooftop or balcony. They are straightforward to grow and very productive in containers. They require large pots (at least 12 inches in height and diameter) but ensure they have one or more drainage holes to release excess water through. Make use of soil mix with good quality, tons of organic matter, and good aeration. If you are planting seeds, fill the container with soil within 1–2 inches of the top, while if you are growing from young plants, fill the container ¾ full. Sow 5 – 6 seeds in each container if you are growing from seed but cut back the plants to two after the seeds sprout. It is generally best to grow one squash plant in each container, and if you are staking your squash, do it before planting, right after filling

the pot with soil. Squashes require 8 hours of sun exposure every day and should be protected from frost and wind. Find a perfect location in your garden where this requirement can be meant and remember to frequently water the soil to stay moist but not marshy.

SWEET CORN OR MAIZE

Corn was at first the common name for oat crops like wheat, grain, oats, and rye. The excellent yellow grain we by and by considering as corn was familiar with Europe by Columbus and individual explorers. The corn plant conveys a tall stalk that yields a couple of ears each. Since corn requires a lot of nitrogen to thrive, it is commonly scattered 12 inches isolated. Regardless, if the corn is given good nitrogen, possible in an aquaponics system, corn can be planted as eagerly as every 6 inches, or four plants for each square foot.

Nearby Americans would plant corn, beans, and squash together and suggested these plants as the Three Sisters. The seeds would pump nitrogen into the soil. The corn would give a tall stalk to the bean plant to climb, and the squash leaves would shield the ground like mulch, with the prickly hairs on the vines ruining bugs. After the plants, dishes were created combining beans and corn. This contributed to diminishing the need to raise family unit animals for sustenance.

Chapter - 30
UNDERSTANDING THE ROLE OF NUTRIENTS

NUTRIENTS FOR THE PLANTS

Nutrients are integral to your success because your plants need to be supplied with food continuously. You can mix your own nutrients in large or small amounts using different formulae. However, the novice should start with a commercially available, premixed nutrient at least until a hydroponic sensation has been established.

In soil farming, nature does a lot of work, although often not completely; otherwise, farmers would not have to use fertilizers. Nearly all soil has nutrients in it, but you take over from nature when you grow hydroponically, and often you can improve the quality of the nutrients supplied.

NUTRIENT SOLUTION

Plants collect the nutrients they need to grow from the soil, and it may have been apparent to you already that water supplies the nutrients in hydroponics. However, water alone doesn't have the 14 nutrients plants require; thus there is the need for nutrient solutions.

The first thing to know about nutrient solutions is that it comes in different ratios. Plants constantly change their requirements as they grow; thus, gardeners can't stick to a single solution throughout. Furthermore, different crops require different nutrient ratios. What will make a tomato crop bloom may not do the same for an orchid.

Nutrient solutions can be bought in hydroponics stores, and their ratios are clearly printed on the bottle's label - the three seemingly random numbers at the bottom (e.g. 2-1-6, 0-5-4, or 5-0-1). Each number stands for the three primary macronutrients, commonly known as NPK or nitrogen (N), phosphorus (P), and potassium (K). Although they are called 'ratios,' these numbers are the percentages of each macronutrient against the entire bottle. Therefore, if the label says, 2-1-6, it means it contains 2% nitrogen, 1% phosphorus, and 6% potassium.

HOMEMADE NUTRIENTS

The most common homemade nutrient is made from salts extracted from fertilizer. Such salts are available in bulk from farm companies, suppliers of plant food, some nurseries, gardening shops, and chemical suppliers. The problem with this approach is that in twenty-five to fifty-pound bags, you generally have to buy some of these salts, and unless you grow in large hydroponic gardens, these amounts will make the whole thing very difficult and expensive.

Besides the three essential elements of nitrogen (N), phosphorus (P), and potassium (K) for all plant growth, your nutrient will contain at least ten trace elements. The following are sulfur, iron, manganese, zinc, copper, boron, magnesium, calcium, molybdenum, chlorine.

As fertilizer for the hydroponic culture, three different forms are used: nutrient salt, liquid fertilizer, or ion exchange fertilizer. Then it is subdivided according to the composition: nitrogen-stressed, phosphorous-retained, potassium-reinforced, etc., depending on the use of plants with special needs. The (normal) regulating fertilizer is slightly potassium-enriched and meets most ornamental and indoor plants' needs. There are also fertilizers that contain only one nutrient or two or three nutrients. It is used when, for a short time or during a particularly needy growth phase (flowering), this single nutrient is needed to an increased extent.

The composition of a (normal) fertilizer is characterized by the three (or four) characters NPK. N is nitrogen (nitrogen), P is phosphorus, K is potassium. Often one finds on the label also the fourth sign mg, and it stands for magnesium. These characters are followed by numbers separated by a hyphen or colon. Example: NPKMG 123162 or 12: 3: 16: 2. In this case, it is the composition, a potassium-stressed fertilizer, which is mostly used for hydroponics. There are other compositions as well. Thus, in the hydroponic commercial horticulture in the first growth phase, a nitrogen-stressed fertilizer is often used in the bloom phase, a phosphorus-rich, and in the fruit phase, a kaliumbetonter. Cacti usually needs a specially made fertilizer, namely a more potassium-stressed (because of the tissue's strong water binding). Another fertilizer contains little or no nitrogen. It is added to the nutrient solution only when the desired pH value has been determined. Namely, it can be influenced by selecting a particular nitrogen fertilizer type of ph. The addition of ammonium allows the lowering of the pH value, which, however, requires experience.

A disadvantage is the use of liquid hydroponic fertilizer and dissolved hydroponic fertilizer, which shortened the vessels' cleaning interval. Part of the fertilizer crystallizes out and settles in expanded clay. This should be rinsed with every renewal of the nutrient solution. Here's a word about so-called fertilizer. There is no artificial fertilizer! This is just the expression of people who lack understanding of manure and fertilizer. One should also speak better of mineral fertilizer.

The nutrient solution consists of water to which all nutrients necessary for plant growth are added. This

sounds easier than it is. At this point, therefore, only the necessary is to be conveyed. Anyone who wants to know exactly can acquire all deepening knowledge under advanced hydroponics.

IRRIGATION WATER

Proper fertilization depends on the particular water quality in each case. Depending on their location or origin, irrigation water may contain varying amounts of both beneficial and undesirable substances (ions). There is, therefore, no patent remedy for the fertilization of "hydroponics" incidentally; this also applies to all other culture processes, including those inorganic substrates. Simplified, the different waters can be divided into the following classes:

- Low salt with low conductivity and low hardness, including rainwater
- Medium salt content and medium hardness
- High salt content and high hardness

The water supply companies provide detailed information on tap water quality, either directly or via the internet. Beware of in-house water softening systems. These change the composition of the tap water considerably. Softened water is unsuitable as water for plants.

Chapter - 31
HOW TO GROW HERBS

A PLANT-BY-PLANT GUIDE TO HERBS

- Basil
- Edible Leaves
- Cool or warm greenhouse

Basil is a beautiful herb with such a gorgeous aroma you wish to increase it yearlong, but outside it's grown as an annual in almost any northern garden. Varieties have a vast selection of tastes like citrus, cinnamon, lemon, and lime. Start sowing in late winter or early spring at the germination room. Proceed to sow through the growing year. Basil requires from three to eight weeks to germinate, based on variety and temperature, but may germinate quickest when temperatures are 65°F (18°C) or warmer.

Transplant seedlings to 4--6. (10--15 cm) pots, 1 plant per pot, at great loamy well-drained potting soil with neutral to slightly acidic pH. Fertilize with a high nitrogen fertilizer to get powerful olive development. Continue on the other side but not let the soil dry outside. Plants are ready to harvest within sixty to eighty times based on temperature and desirable leaf size. Snip tops off to get rid of seeds and maintain foliage production moving. Basil can create downy mold or Fusarium wilt if rainwater temperatures drop below 50°F (10°C). Whiteflies may also be an insect at the greenhouse.

- Bay laurel
- Evergreen shrub or tree
- Leaves used for seasoning
- Propagate from trick
- Cool or hot greenhouse

Occasionally referred to as sweet bay, this blossom plant ought to be in each greenhouse. It's simple to develop, needs very little care, also leaves can easily be ripped off when required. Outdoors the plant could rise to 40 ft. (12 m), however at the greenhouse, it ought to be trained as a tree. Varieties contain willow leaf laurel (Laurus nobilis'Angustifolia'), L. nobilis'Aurea' with yellowish foliage, also wavy-leafed laurel (L. nobilis'Undulata'). Plant little footprints in 1 gal. (4 liter) containers, in well-drained potting soil with additional compost for a long term, fertilizing, and weed up because the plant grows bigger. Proceed when all risk of frost has passed. Throughout the summertime, fertilize lightly using a balanced fertilizer. Bay can readily be pruned to keep it in form. It'll shed a few leaves once transferred to the greenhouse in fall, but this is natural. This plant is generally trouble-free, however, look outside for fire blight on branch hints.

TRENDY GREENHOUSE

Chamomile is a somewhat simple perennial herb to increase and is thought to have a calming effect when drunk as a tea. Just crazy chamomile (Matricaria recutita) and Roman, German, or English chamomile (Chamaemelum nobile) should be used in teas. Sow seeds at shallow 6 in. (15 cm) strands in well-drained sandy loam with loads of mulch; seeds may emerge in ten days to a couple of weeks. Keep the soil moist until seedlings germinate.

Transfer the baskets apart since the plant leaves disperse and hang the bud. Plants grow about 8 in. (20 cm) tall and over 15 in. (37 cm) broad. It may take two to 3 weeks for the crops to grow to harvestable size together with blossoms. Generally trouble-free.

- Chervil
- Anthriscus cerefolium
- Edible leaves
- Cool greenhouse

Old chervil seed doesn't germinate well; however, a new seed may germinate in six to eight weeks. Chervil is extremely simple to develop, but it's very long taproot (it's a part of the carrot family) takes a deep kettle. Chervil can grow in most soils. Give plants lots of water. Harvest leaves when the plant is big enough. Following four to eight months, chervil will blossom, and the leaves will soon create a sweeter flavor. Plants can go to seed in warm weather. Control aphids.

- Chives
- Allium schoenoprasum
- Perennial from bulbs
- Edible leaves and flowers
- Branch from bulbs
- Cool Greenhouse
- Full sun or part shade

Additionally, known as chives, all these are members of the family. Chinese chives (Allium tuberosum) are alike but have white blossoms. Leaves die down in the winter months once the bulbs require a period of cold. Sow seeds in containers; they take approximately a week to germinate. Continue to develop the chives in 4--6 months. (10--15 cm) pots or transplant them into the backyard, where they're decorative enough to function as edging plants within a blossom border.

Chives prefer loamy, well-drained soil with a great deal of compost. Harvest the leaves and blossoms to be used in salads and as a garnish. To promote the plants to generate additional bulbs, slough off the seed heads. Finally, even tiny clumps grow very big and could be raised and divided. Generally trouble-free.

Chapter - 32
HOW TO GROW FRUITS PLANTS

A PLANT-BY-PLANT GUIDE TO GREENHOUSE FRUIT

- Avocado
- Persea Americana
- Evergreen Tree
- Grow out of grafted plants
- Tropical or subtropical greenhouse

At the same point or another, most of us have attempted to develop an avocado out of a pit. The outcome is frequently a tall stem of a plant which won't bear fruit after five or six decades of growth. The best method to acquire an avocado that may fruit is to purchase a respectable dealer's grafted cultivar. (You may even graft a branch out of a fruiting tree on the rootstock which you grew out of a seed) Many nurseries market'Haas' or Mexican 'Fuerte' cultivars. Typically, you'll have to purchase two crops and cross-legged to acquire a fantastic fruit set, or you might have the ability to purchase a tree using 2 different branches to cross-legged. But some grape trees, notably'Haas'fruit, ardently only another calendar year. Purchase the cultivar that will be appropriate for the night temperature of your greenhouse. Some forms can return to as much as 25°F (-4°C), however, returns endure. Ensure the bud for the avocado is big enough. Use moist, fertile soil with a lot of organic matter. Give loads of water, but don't enable the plant to sit in water. Feed having a high-nitrogen fertilizer early in the summertime. Once collected, you're able to hasten ripening by placing the fruit into a purse with a couple of apples. A mature tree may provide you twenty-five to thirty each year, but nevertheless, it might take ten to twelve years for that dimension. Generally trouble-free.

BANANA AND PLANTAIN

Musa Perennial Grow from branches in tropical or subtropical climates. There are several hundred types of banana and plantains, a lot of them inedible. But banana crops are appealing for your greenhouse or conservatory, even in the event that you don't receive the fruit. I also harvest banana leaves to wrap grilled poultry and pork and make other succulent banana-flavored dishes. Unless you've got a massive greenhouse, it is a fantastic idea to purchase rainbow varieties such as 'Super Dwarf Cavendish.' Occasionally it almost sounds as though you're able to observe the banana plant growth; foliage can grow. (7.5 cm) within 1 day. To encourage this speedy development, simmer banana crops while temperatures are hot. Plant in well-drained land high in humus, dirt, and lavender. Bananas slow their expansion under a minimum of 75--80°F (24--27°C). Inside my heated greenhouse that the plant stops growing across mid-autumn. It took five years to get my very first banana plant to achieve maturity and specify a stem of fruit from midsummer.

It set the initial six"palms" of peanuts, but as temperatures dropped, the covers fell from the fruiting spathe. In my greenhouse, the carrots won't ripen before the summer once the temperature climbs again. Most resources suggest harvesting your peanuts by lopping from the spathe. However, I have discovered that the batter ripens in the surface down, therefore cutting off a hand at one time prolongs the crop. After harvesting, then cut the whole fruiting stem at ground level. (It is quite fibrous, and that means you have to dip it into little pieces before placing it in the compost). The banana origin lays out fresh shoots, occasionally called suckers. Every one of these may be chopped off the older root and brightens up. The stem includes layers; each layer ends in a leaf. Since the plant develops, the ground leaves die away and have to get cut back again. The best approach to do is use a sharp knife having a blade at 8. (20 cm) long.

- Star fruit
- Deciduous tree
- Grow from container crops
- Tropical or Subtropical Greenhouse

The major carambola (starfruit) is'Arkin'; however, there are different kinds ('Golden Star', 'Newcomb,' also Thayer's) with veggies that vary from sour to reasonably sweet. If at all possible, taste a few fruit prior to choosing your cultivar. It requires a lot of water and higher humidity but doesn't like to get flooded. Founded in abundant well-drained loam, mixed with vermiculite or perlite; pH has to be somewhat acidic. Fertilize throughout the growing season using a 10-5-10 fertilizer every 2 weeks or so.

When the leaves turn yellow, the plant might be chlorotic, and also, you ought to feel it using liquid chelated iron. Leave the fruit into the tree till it's ripe--normally midwinter to late winter. Choose it with caution, since it's easily damaged. Slice starfruit and then increase your favorite fruit salads or just consume it out of hand.

- Citrus
- Evergreen tree
- Growing in container plants
- Warm greenhouse

Citrus is one of their preferred plants for home farmers. In spring, the blossoms smell fantastic. In the winter, oranges and may be chosen directly from the tree. There are several different citruses to your greenhouse, by the little Calamondin orange (Citrus mitis) and Meyer or even Ponderosa (C. limon 'Meyer,' C. limon 'Ponderosa'), to bigger Mexican (Essential) (C. aurantifolia) and Mexican lime. You might even develop Cara navel oranges (C. sinensis), mandarins like the seedless 'Kishu,' also kumquats (Fortunella margarita). Founded in abundant well-drained loam, mixed with vermiculite or perlite, citrus takes some time to develop to a fruiting dimension. Every year you'll have to improve the size of this marijuana before your trees are near to grow. The majority of my own five-year-old trees come in 24 in. (60 cm) containers whereas the trees (a few are old) have been at 30 in. (76 cm) pots.

Citrus blossoms in spring, and if you do not have bees in the greenhouse, you'll need to hand pollinate using a paintbrush. It is normal for citrus to place and then discards a good deal of little fruit if less than 10% of veggies grow to adulthood, you might want to pollinate more attentively or boost the temperature at the

greenhouse. Citrus needs to be fertilized monthly all summertime with a high-nitrogen feed, for example, 10-5-5. When the leaves turn yellow, iron chlorosis is an indication, and you'll have to feed every day with chelated iron. While I transfer my trees on the terrace in spring, I always squirt them with a chelated iron mix and use a fungicide to eliminate sooty mold, typically deposited by whiteflies from the winter. Bring them inside the greenhouse prior to the first frosts; the fruit ought to grow from early winter to midwinter. Watch for aphids, orange scale, mealybugs, and whitefly.

Chapter - 33
THE DIFFERENCE BETWEEN GROWING IN THE GROUND AND GROWING IN CONTAINERS

If you have ever attempted to germinate seeds grow cuttings onto a windowsill, you are going to love what a pleasure it is to execute these jobs on your greenhouse. With ample space, the appropriate temperatures, controlled light, and constant humidity, plant propagation can be quite simple. Most anglers start with only growing plants from seed; however, the greenhouse is really a nice workspace for all sorts of plant propagation, such as cuttings, division, grafting, and sometimes even plant.

Perennial seeds have been sown in autumn to deceive them into believing they have passed through the whole winter to make them flower the spring; perennials that began in spring typically do not flower the first year. The single perennial vegetable that has to be sown in autumn would be an artichoke. It, also should consider it has passed through chilly to place flower buds (artichoke heads) from spring. Annual vegetables like peppers, eggplants that germinate and develop gradually are found in midwinter.

SEED-STARTING CONTAINERS

Originally, seed-sowing may be completed in plastic apartments, which might or might not be broken into different cells. When the time is for seedlings to be turned out to marginally bigger individual containers, then I would rather utilize square strands. They've a bigger quantity than around pots and if they're placed closely together, water doesn't spill into the distances between them with round pots.

- Plastic pots may be reused several times, provided that you clean them between applications. Most good anglers will conserve and reuse their baskets. Most garden centers may even accept old plastic containers for recycling. If you're worried about plastic waste, nevertheless, you will find other seed-starting containers. The majority of them are produced from biodegradable substances to be utilized both for seeds and for ultimate transplanting, grass and all, in the backyard or greenhouse beds.
- Clay containers are inclined to be around, plus they lose moisture quickly through the bud walls. I prefer

not to utilize these to germinate seedlings since they dry out quite fast and, being little, might require watering or twice two times every day. You should like to use clay pots, bear this in mind while you increase your seeds.

- Paper containers can readily be produced from paper around approximately 6. (15 cm) in diameter.) Should you make them considerably bigger than this, the soil's burden induces the kettle to fall apart. Heavy watering of newspaper baskets may make them glow. But should you begin seeds in paper baskets, your seedlings can readily be implanted into the earth without needing to remove them in the bud. I've made paper baskets from old paper wrapped around a 3. (7.5 cm) paint could. Only wrap pieces of paper around the baskets and fold the ends of this paper on the shade's base.
- Peat trays and baskets are all biodegradable containers made out of peat moss and wood pulp that divide when implanted in the floor. Virtually all of the advertisements for peat pots claim you could plant the bud on the floor, and the plant roots will increase throughout the bud walls. My experience (and that of several anglers I have talked to) is that it requires a minimum of one time for plant roots to grow throughout the bud walls, and also, the ideal approach to transplant these baskets would be to split the marijuana apart once you plant outside.
- Coir containers are created from peat-free coconut fibers, which maintain moisture and divide nicely in the backyard. These containers are extremely sparse, and roots can easily penetrate the bud walls. Their usage is getting more extensive by anglers that have environmental concerns regarding peat.
- Seed pellets seem like little flat pills. The pellet is coated using a nice plastic mesh to maintain the peat moss or soil set up and permit moisture to the medium. Soaking them in plain water for around half an hour leads to the pellet enlarging to approximately 2. (5 cm) tall. When the strands have enlarged, you plant your own seeds in a depression on the surface of the pellet. After the plant has increased, the whole pellet may be seeded to the floor at which the plant roots may spread. But, I've discovered residue of this fine mesh vinyl in the backyard after a year and want to eliminate them when placing it out.

CONTAINERS FOR POTTING UP

As seedlings develop, you re them to successively larger containers. It's possible to grow them to maturity in containers or, even when they've grown big enough to live from the floor, plant them either in the greenhouse or, even when the conditions are correct, into the backyard. Space is at a premium in many greenhouses and shelves may easily become full of plants. The large benefit of growing crops to maturity at a container would be the soil could be precisely suited to this plant. Many specialty crops, like and bromeliads, have exacting dirt conditions. Even vegetables may react to various land types.

Carrots, for instance, demand loose sandy dirt to grow nicely, whereas brassicas desire a rich loam. The

single plant entries in this publication give more info about the soil demands of plants. Pots also offer you flexibility that planting on the floor can't. They are sometimes put near together while the crops are little and proceeded further apart as crops grow.

Ornamental plants that remain in the rainwater yearlong could be implanted in ornamental baskets provided that the strands drain well. You may even replicate the plants to reveal them into their very best attitude or maybe to secure more sunshine on either side or another.

- Clay is your gardener's conventional bud substance; however, unglazed clay (terracotta) will become sterile and fractures easily, particularly if the strands are permitted to suspend or exposed to high-temperature swings. Glazed pots perform marginally better, however, they still violate relatively easily. (If this occurs, save the shards to put in the base of different strands when repotting to assist boost drainage). Occasionally an unsightly white residue may form on the exterior of the skillet. This stems from additives dissolved in the dirt that migrate throughout the clay or even out of tough water. The snowy crust could be washed. In case the bud is overwatered, in addition, it can develop moss on the exterior. However, too, it can easily be washed off. Despite the drawbacks, many anglers enjoy clay pots. Their depth can help to medium temperature swings along with the porosity allows water and air to penetrate in the kettle at which the fine roots in the edge of the root ball may utilize it. Water may also move in another direction away from the roots when the kettle is overwatered. This attribute may be utilized to benefit from crops like cactus that enjoy well-drained soil.
- Air baskets are plastic containers which have perforations at the sides. They were initially created for growing trees together with the concept that the tree root ball wouldn't rise in circles around the base of the bud, a frequent problem that contributes to root-bound plants. They can be found in sizes as small as 1 gal. (4 liters).
- Grow bags are extremely beneficial in the greenhouse, particularly for veggies. Some garden centers offer vinyl build totes pre-filled using soil, frequently with compost mixed into the ground. You might even purchase unfilled luggage—as I do and fill yourself using just the ideal mix. These might be made from cloth, burlap, plastic, or felt-like material. Pre-filled development bags are perfect for crops that don't have deep root systems, such as salad greens, peppers, peppers, eggplant, etc. Deeper mature bags are perfect for plants like which fill the tote with origins as the plant develops. In the event, you utilize mature bags, make certain that there are a couple of drainage holes punched in the base of the tote, even though most bags offered for this purpose include holes punched in them.
- Repurposed containers could be nearly anything, from half of an hour barrels to utilized olive oil tins. Just make certain the kettle has enough drainage and is hardly enough to support the weight of all these plants and dirt it will include.

SOIL AND POTTING SOIL

If it has to do with potting soil, lots of greenhouse anglers have their own tastes. Most commercial growth combinations contain some blend of soil bark, peat moss, compost, humus, sand, perlite or vermiculite, coir, gypsum, dolomitic tone, and even fertilizers. For seed beginning and cuttings, search for a distinctive seed-starting or flashing medium formulated particularly for the crops you're sowing or dispersing. When left to dry, then a potting soil might become difficult and invisible, and it is going not to absorb water till it's thoroughly soaked. Potting mixes for container plants frequently contain wetting agents—polymer pellets which maintain water and release it gradually.

Soils with wetting agents could be watered less frequently without wastage of water and therefore are used for hanging baskets or window boxes. Specialty potting mixtures are offered for many plant types. For example, a mix meant for container plants might get a better proportion of water-retentive peat moss or coir compared to a mix that's intended only for seed starting. After experimenting with many combinations, my taste is an expert growing mixture I buy in sterile compressed bales in the wholesaler. It's just the ideal consistency to become wetted, it moves in the pots readily, and I've had excellent results out of it using the two seedlings and potted plants. I accommodate the mixture to match certain plants. For example, if I desire a cactus planting mix, I blend in 25 percent vermiculite and 25 to 50 percent sand. For growing plants such as fruit shrubs and trees from massive containers, I utilize 40 percent potting soil, 20% sand or vermiculite, and 40 percent mulch, using a 1. (25 mm) layer of compacted soil on top to function as compost and retain any weeds in check.

It is also possible to create your own container potting mix utilizing screened garden loam, mulch, along with a lightening agent like vermiculite or perlite. Some anglers include peat moss or sand for superior drainage, together with some slow-release fertilizer. Should you create your own potting mix, then the greatest difficulty will be marijuana seeds which come in the garden dirt or mulch?

POTTING UP

Placing your seedlings at a bigger pot as soon as they've germinated is called potting up or down on. To weed up, gently raise the expanding plantlet in the seed (loosen the dirt and wait from the foliage, so you don't hurt the stem) and place it into a bigger pot.

If you're starting berries, place them deeper into the pit than they had been growing. The buried portion of this stem will become roots. The other plants ought to be replanted at precisely the exact same level since they were initially growing. Following a couple of days beneath lights to allow the plant to detect its origins and to speak, you are able to move your plants from the germination room and to the greenhouse.

Chapter - 34
LIST OF 60 FRUITS AND VEGETABLES TO GROW IN A GREENHOUSE

According to the USDA, in the winter of 2012-2013, 50% of all produce was imported from other countries. Even with produce grown in season, it can be difficult to have a variety without a greenhouse or at least some formal protection. Greenhouses are a great way to have fresh produce year-round. The following are fruits and vegetables commonly available at grocery stores and specialty markets that can be grown in a greenhouse. Some of the listings include fruit or vegetable varieties. All varieties have been confirmed by seed companies, farmers, or growers. Varieties not confirmed by at least two sources are not included. Most items listed have been verified by multiple sources, however, some varieties may be new to the market and there are not yet enough sources to verify that they grow well in a greenhouse or can even be grown at all. For this reason, many of the fruits and vegetables in this list are labeled as "not verified," but we can happily confirm that you will enjoy success with them. Greenhouses vary in size and shape, so some of the varieties may need to be adjusted to fit your growing space. Please note that the listed varieties are not specifically meant to be grown in a greenhouse for some of these items. The list will grow as we get more feedback and research.

- Anise
- Apples
- Apricots
- Arugula
- Asparagus
- Avocados
- Bananas
- Basil
- Bay laurel
- Beans
- Begonia
- Broccoli
- Brussels Sprouts
- Bush Beans
- Cabbage
- Cantaloupe

- Carrots
- Catnip
- Celery
- Cilantro
- Collard Greens
- Corn
- Cucumbers
- Cumin
- Cherries
- Chilies
- Eggplant
- Grapes
- Honeydew Melon
- Kalanchoe
- Kale
- Kiwifruit
- Lavender
- Lima Beans
- Mangos
- Mint
- Nigellia
- Okra
- Onions
- Parsnips
- Peaches
- Pears
- Peas
- Pepper
- Pineapples
- Plums
- Radishes
- Raspberry
- Rhubarb
- Rosemary
- Sage
- Salad greens
- Smooth Cayenne
- Spinach
- Strawberries
- Tarragon
- Thyme
- Watermelon
- Zucchini

The ugli fruit is a cross between a tangerine and an orange, which guarantees you get both the tart and sweet flavors of both fruits in one bite. This makes them very popular in Caribbean countries where they're grown in large quantities, and citrus fruits aren't as readily available, so they are an excellent

crop to grow if your climate isn't warm enough for orange trees or other citrus crops. They are self-pollinating, so they don't require a second tree to bear fruit. They also have a tendency to grow very large, so you should have plenty of room in your greenhouse for them. The trees don't take long to grow or produce fruit, and as they're hardy plants that can withstand cold temperatures, they're an excellent choice for greenhouse growers who live in cooler climates. They're incredibly easy to grow and care for, so if you're new to gardening and want an easy fruit tree to start out with, the Ugli Fruit is a great option.

Watermelons do best when the temperature is at least 85 degrees Fahrenheit, but they can grow in temperatures up to 100 degrees without any problem. If you live in a warm climate and want to grow your own watermelons, then it's best to choose an early-bearing variety that doesn't require a lot of time to mature. You can choose a hybrid variety that's meant for outdoor growing if you have room for them outside, but they will grow large and take up quite a bit of room. They're easy plants to care for if you use mulch around the plant's base as it prevents weeds from growing underneath it, which is why you should avoid using plastic or polyester mulches around watermelons as they trap water under themselves instead of letting them filter through into the soil.

Caring for your greenhouse garden can be a full-time job if you do it right, but it's absolutely worth the effort in the end as you can have your own tasty produce that's grown locally and often more sweet or juicy than other fruits and vegetables from stores. All you need to get started is some seeds, soil, pots, and a greenhouse in which to grow them. Before you know it, you will have your own fresh produce that you can eat or give away to family members and friends!

Chapter - 35
IDENTIFY PEST AND DISEASE IN YOUR GREENHOUSE AND KNOW HOW TO COMBAT THEM

Here is where the information you gathered comes into play. Without the information, you might think that you need to act quickly and get rid of the pests. Time to bring in the big guns! However, what you should be doing is analyzing the situation properly. Do you see pests restricted to a particular plant or spreading out in your garden? Even if these creatures are spread out, do you notice them in few numbers, or do you see hundreds of them?

This process is known as establishing damage thresholds. It basically means that you are trying to measure the extent of pest growth in your garden before taking reactive measures.

If you have a small number of pests, you can think about using one of the solutions below. However, if the pests have multiplied to a considerable amount, then it might be time to introduce the big guns (and by that, I mean pesticides).

CHOOSE YOUR CONTROL METHOD

After getting the necessary information and concluding how severe the pest problem is, you can choose various control methods to deal with the problem.

PHYSICAL CONTROL METHODS

If pests are getting to your crops, then you could try physically keeping them away. There are a number of ways to do this. Here are a few:

ERECTING BARRIERS

Call this your initial defense plan. By setting up barriers, you can prevent pests from actually reaching your plants. A good example could be a fence, which is great for keeping away rodents and animals such as cats (yes, our feline friends can be pests, too). To protect against birds, you could use bird netting. Wire meshes and other forms of netting may be able to protect your crops from flying insects. When you become aware of what insect or animal causes your garden a lot of distress, you can choose an appropriate physical barrier.

GETTING HANDY

Many farmers and gardeners simply choose to use their hands to pick away the pests if they are large bugs and creatures such as snails. This is an inexpensive and non-toxic method of getting rid of your creature's problem. However, if you feel squeamish about working with your hands, there are many bug vacuums on the market to help you do the job.

USING WATER

If you discover small creatures inhabiting your garden without your permission, then you can easily get rid of them with a spray or stream of water. Simply bring your hose to your plants, turn on the water and dislodge these nasty critters. In addition to removing pests, you end watering the plants as well. However, do make sure that you do not use a lot of water. You might end up drowning the plants.

EXAMINE YOUR PLANTS

It is crucial to inspect all your plants before bringing them to the greenhouse to avoid the spreading of bugs inside. Just as crops and flowers like the warmness of a greenhouse so do pests and they increase rapidly in the heat. Therefore, ensure to thoroughly scrutinize any new plants for signs of larvae or insects on the stem or leaves before taking them in.

STERILIZE YOUR TOOLS

A good number of gardeners will often use the same tools all around the garden, moving them around the lawn, compost heap, vegetable patch, flower beds, shed, and greenhouse. This implies that they can easily pick up bugs from the soil outdoors and infect the plants inside the building. So to be very cautious, you will want to give your trowels, spades, and other equipment a good clean after every use. Soaking them in soapy water will do well.

ELIMINATE EVERY SOURCE OF STANDING WATER

Standing water is favorable to the increase of pests and diseases, so ensure there is no source of stagnant water around and inside the greenhouse. Be it puddle or jug; get rid of every single source of water.

ISOLATE YOUR NEW PLANTS

Your greenhouse might be free from pests, but new plants can turn out to be buggy. As soon as possible, the new plants can infest your whole greenhouse with pests. To avoid this scenario, you may need to put your new plants in an isolation chamber until you confirm they're pest-free. You may make use of an aquarium with a tight-fitting cover if you do not have an isolation chamber.

ADDING REPELLANTS

You can also utilize certain substances that pests do not come close to. For your typical garden pests, you can make use of special oils or scents. Look for any repellant that matches the pest that is currently attacking your garden. Oh, and by the way, by repellant, I don't mean a bug repellant!

CREATING TRAPS

Traps work well because they are unexpected. They are designed to either lure a creature towards it or catch them unaware. A common example is the spring-loaded trap for catching mice. There are numerous traps for different scenarios, such as glue traps, electronic traps, and more. Find the one that suits your needs.

BIOLOGICAL CONTROL METHODS

Under these control methods, you are using a living organism to take care of the more dangerous organisms in your garden. Typically, this would mean using creatures beneficial to your garden (as we had seen some examples earlier). However, in this case, we are also considering substances that have useful bacteria or fungi to apply to the plants. These substances have a repelling effect. They prevent the pest from approaching your plants.

Chapter - 36
SIMPLE TIPS TO HELP PROTECT YOUR CROPS AGAINST DISEASES

However, what might sound like a frightening scenario can typically be solved by taking a few precautionary steps. If all else fails and you still would like to consider using sprays, then do not worry.

The thing about pesticides is that they have an instant (and noticeable) effect. You can see the number of pests on your plants reduced. Nevertheless, there are certain effects in the long term – such as depleting the health of your soil and slightly poisoning your water – that might prove disastrous for you in the future. You might have to change the soil entirely. If you are using a raised bed, then this might not be a problem. However, if you have decided to plant directly into the earth, then getting rid of all that pesticide residue is a strenuous process.

Here is another thing that you should keep in mind; sometimes, getting rid of the pests may not be necessary. If you have aphids roaming around on your plants, then see if you have helpful insects that dine on these aphids. In fact, certain farmers are known to let the pests live. This is because they usually have some form of predator that can take care of the pest problem. This has two beneficial results:

You do not have to spend time (and money on pest control activities in some situations).

You let someone (or something) else take care of the problem for you. A friend in need is a friend indeed. Even if that friend just happens to have four legs, wings, or antennae.

Another thing to keep in mind; your problem might not be related to pests. It is easy to think that certain creatures have wreaked havoc on your lovely garden. Actually, it is certainly tempting to think that way. However, in many cases, the situation might just be because of other factors. Is there enough moisture for the plants? Are strong winds causing harm to them? Was there heavy rainfall recently? Did it hail? Even water pollution could be another factor to consider. You see, all of these factors cause unnecessary stress on the plants, which further begins to attract the pests in your area. Trying to get to the root of the problem might help you effectively remove the pests without using any pest control techniques (including pesticides).

In IPM, farmers and gardeners take gradually stronger steps to get rid of the pests in their garden. They start by working on the conditions that help the growth of the crops. Are these conditions beneficial? Do the crops have everything they need? Once they are able to work around these conditions, they seek to establish a level of damage they can accept. Once that is done, they move on to using methods that have minimal toxicity. If that does not work, they begin using toxic or invasive methods.

- **JOIN THE RESISTANCE!**

The first thing that you should do is focus on creating pest resistant plants. You see, gardeners and farmers often work with a plethora of plant species. Some of these plants have some unique traits. One of those unique traits is the ability of the plant to have disease resistance. This means that the plant suffers minimal damage from a specific disease, similar to how the human immune system builds resistance against diseases.

Many of the modern plants have built resistance to many diseases that could cause considerable damage. What's more, you can find plants that also have resistance to certain insects. For example, you can find special types of squash that can keep away certain types of beetles. This might help you effectively find a solution against these pests without having to resort to other methods of pest control.

In fact, when you are purchasing plants, you might receive information about what pests those plants resist. After knowing what pests are common in your area, you can match the plant to that particular pest.

- **INVITING LESS PESTS**

While you might be confident that you have taken all the precautionary steps to keep away pests, there might be certain reasons your garden is still attracting those nasty critters.

What you can do to avoid this situation is to plant your crops in small batches throughout your garden. Then you can add other plants into the mix (preferably those that have resistance against the pests in your area). This confuses the insects, tricking them into believing that perhaps your garden does not have the food they are looking for. Additionally, you might be able to avoid diseases from spreading when you mix plant breeds.

- **MAKE FRIENDS WITH CREATURES**

I am not asking you to invite creatures into your house for tea and supper. What I mean is to allow the growth of certain organisms that could help you get rid of pests. For example, certain types of spiders leave your plants alone, but find abundant food in the pests that might live there. You can always encourage the growth of these pest-hunters, as you can call them.

INSECTICIDES

These are a form of pesticide that are specifically made to harm, eliminate, or repel one or more species of insect. You can discover insecticides in various forms such as sprays, gels, and even traps. Pick one based on the pest that is attacking your garden.

Once you have selected your insecticide, it is better to know the below tips:

- I would recommend using just one type of insecticide in your garden. Adding two or more insecticides diminishes their effect and may inadvertently cause harm to your garden.
- Remember that not all insecticides take the same time to remove pests from your garden. You might have to wait longer for certain types.
- Try to see if you really need the spray. For example, if you want to get rid of ants, you could use a bait instead (after all, ants are attracted to nearby sources of food).

FUNGICIDES

These are pesticides that are made to kill fungal infections on the plants and any fungi spores that might have latched onto your crops. In some cases, fungicides are used to mitigate the effects of mildew and mold. The way they function is by damaging either the fungal cell structure or stopping the energy production in cells.

When you are ready to use your fungicide, do make note of the below tips:

In many cases, people might accidentally diagnose fungal diseases for their plants when in reality, it might not be a disease at all. Make sure you use the help of local experts to give you a second opinion. They might just prevent you from buying a fungicide needlessly and might recommend another solution.

- Make sure that leaves are not kept wet for too long. Simply keeping the leaves dry after watering them helps reduce the spread of fungi.
- Keep your tools sanitized. Sometimes, the fungi could spread from one plant to another because they stuck to the tools you were using.

HERBICIDES

The main purpose of herbicides in a garden is to get rid of all the weeds.

When you have gotten your herbicide, do make note of the following tips:

- Always make sure that the instructions on the herbicide suit your purposes.
- Go easy on its application. Adding more herbicides might sound like a safe bet, but it might end up damaging your plants. If you feel unsure, read the instructions provided on the herbicide to understand its usage quantity.
- Certain herbicides show immediate results. Others take a while to get rid of the weeds. Always check with the seller or supplier for details before using the herbicide. This way, you are not left wondering if you had bought a defective product when you see weeds present even after the third day of using the herbicide.

Chapter - 37
DEALING WITH THE POTENTIAL DISEASES AND PEST YOU WOULD ENCOUNTER IN YOUR GREENHOUSE

PEST CONTROL - MANAGING PESTS

The term pest control often conjures up images of people using sprays filled with chemicals. You might think that using such methods is rather extreme. However, what might sound like a frightening scenario can typically be solved by taking a few precautionary steps. If all other methods fail and you still want to consider using sprays, then don't worry.

You might have to change the soil entirely. If you are using a raised bed, then this might not be a problem. However, if you have decided to plant directly into the earth, then getting rid of all that pesticide residue is a strenuous process.

However, in many cases, the situation might just be because of other factors. Is there enough moisture for the plants? Are strong winds causing harm to them? Was there heavy rainfall recently? Did it hail? Even water pollution could be another factor to consider. You see, all of these factors cause unnecessary stress on the plants, which further begins to attract the pests in your area. Trying to get to the root of the problem might help you effectively remove the pests without using any pest control techniques (including pesticides).

The idea behind evaluating your garden is to know what kind of problem you are dealing with. That may help you decide if you would like to head over to the step, which is the integrated pest management, or 'IPM' for short, process.

They start by working on the conditions that help the growth of the crops. Are these conditions beneficial? Do the crops have everything they need? Once they are able to work around these conditions, they seek to establish a level of damage they can accept. Once that is done, they move on to using methods that have minimal toxicity. If that does not work, they begin using toxic or invasive methods.

PLANT CONDITIONS

Make sure you have placed the plant in the right spot, based on how much water, sunlight, and essential nutrients that the plant may require. This is because stress begins to affect those plants that do not receive what they require. Stress, in turn, causes plants to release certain chemicals in the air, which are like beacons for all the pests in the area. Humans might deal with stress through many means. Plants, however, do not have mechanisms to resist stress. They eventually begin to experience deteriorating health and finally succumb to the effects of pests. This does not mean that healthy plants cannot attract pests, but they are capable of surviving attacks when an unhealthy plant may not be able to.

MIXED PLANTS

Most insects have receptors that allow them to target their favorite plants. It is how bees can seek out nectar so easily. If you have the plants that insects are waiting to attack and you have done nothing to protect those plants, then you might as well schedule buffet hours for the insects! What you can do to avoid this situation is to plant your crops in small batches throughout your garden. Then you can add other plants into the mix (preferably those that have resistance against the pests in your area). This confuses the insects, tricking them into believing that perhaps your garden does not have the food they are looking for. Additionally, you might be able to avoid diseases from spreading when you mix plant breeds.

TIMING

Certain pests often arrive during certain climates. This fact might give you an idea of the kind of threat you are dealing with. When plants are young, they do not have the strength to ward off pests effectively, which is why you can plant your crops early so that your crops have strong tissues by the time the pest climate arrives. In some cases, insects often leave eggs behind in gardens. When the larvae hatch, they find a ready source of food in the plants around them. For this reason, you could also plant your crops a few weeks after the larvae have hatched, allowing you to starve the pests before working on your garden.

Here is a pro tip: speak to farmers in your area about the emergence of pests. They have extensive knowledge about when these pests might come out during a particular season, allowing you to know how long to wait before planting your crops.

CROP ROTATION

You can move around the crops to new locations in your greenhouse each year. This does not give pests a particular spot to target. Shifting locations confuses the pests, who might be used to finding plants in a specific spot of the garden. Certain insects often lay their eggs in one location when they realize that they know where they can find a ready supply of food. However, by moving your crops around, larvae that hatch might not find their food source. Before they can discover food, they might starve and you might be able to get rid of them without much effort. Do note that crop rotation is most commonly possible with annual plants, when they can be cycled year after year. Perennial plants are usually harvested after one year, so they cannot be quickly rotated. So make a note of this when you plan to change plant locations in your garden.

GO EASY ON THE FERTILIZER

This might be a common mistake committed by beginners. Gardeners who are starting out might worry about the amount of fertilizer that they use. Many use too much to avoid using too little. Unfortunately, too much fertilizer can cause harm to plants, just the way too little can. In fact, you could say that increasing the amount of fertilizer to a plant is like giving steroids to them! For example, soil nutrients provide nitrogen to the plant. This is good in moderate quantities. By adding more fertilizer, you increase the supply of nitrogen. Providing excess amounts of nitrogen might cause rapid growth in plants. This causes them to end up being juicy. This might not sound all that bad. Who doesn't love juicy food? You and every other multi-legged creature will be waiting to get a bite out of those plants. Pests might become attracted to the unnatural growth, finding a rich source of food for them and their offspring.

CLEAN UP OTHER MATERIALS

If you notice fallen leaves, fruits, or other objects in your garden that should not typically be there, then make sure you clear them out. These objects and debris might carry organisms and pests on them that could be transferred to your plants. This increases the chances of infecting your plants with diseases or sending pests into their midst. Once you have cleaned up, see if you can also cultivate the soil when you get the opportunity. This reveals any hidden pest eggs. Additionally, if there are any larvae, you might just let predators (or even the weather) get rid of them.

CONCLUSION

Thank you for taking the time to read this. We hope it was helpful to you in starting your greenhouse gardening journey!

Here are some other things that might be of interest for beginners:

A greenhouse has different zones with different climates. The equatorial zone is hot and humid because of the amount of sunlight that it receives, whilst the polar regions are cold so as not to melt plants during the winter months. As a beginner, you should pick one or two zones that are suitable for your plants' needs.

Heat and light are important. Thousands of plants are grown for the purpose of producing seeds and flowers. They need to perform this process; therefore, they need heat, light, and water. If you have a well-ventilated greenhouse, you could grow your own peppers and tomatoes during summer.

If you own a greenhouse, then you know that they require much work. You might be wondering how to take care of it. You must check if there are any leaks in the roof, walls, or windows. If you notice any problems, you need to solve them as quickly as possible because that is the first step towards ensuring that your greenhouse lasts for a long time.

Just because you have a greenhouse doesn't mean that you should stop your usual gardening activities! You still have to do things such as fertilizing, weeding, pruning, and feeding your plants until they reach maturity.

If you have any leftover plants and seeds from the previous season, you should start your greenhouse gardening with them. You can grow your own herbs, flowers, and vegetables so that they can be used for cooking. You might even want to give your friends and neighbors a few of the plants as gifts.

To create a more efficient environment within your greenhouse, you need to plant both heat lovers and cool lovers plants within different zones. That way, you will get the best out of what your plants can offer.

In most greenhouses, there are few windows that let in natural light for the plants to use for photosynthesis. You can widen the windows and use transparent materials for them. You might want to use large plastic sheets that are used for covering things like boats or cars.

When you are building your greenhouse, it's important that you make sure that it is strong enough to

withstand a storm or high winds. You don't want any of your plants or yourself to get injured because of the greenhouse collapsing under pressure.

When you have finished building your greenhouse and when it is time for you to begin growing plants, make sure that you place them on soil beds that are watered regularly with compost teas made in containers, water from your rainwater collector, or plant saps. You should also check the soil and water regularly.

It's not always fun to use synthetic pesticides, which is why many people choose to grow their own vegetables and flowers. When growing plants indoors, the organic fertilizer you use will be directly absorbed into the roots. Plants that are grown in a greenhouse are also protected from pests and diseases because of the lack of food and lighting for them to breed.

You should have an automatic watering system for your greenhouse in order to ensure that your plants stay healthy and aren't dry when they need water the most, especially during hot summers.

You should put mirrors up within your greenhouse because they reflect heat back at plants. In addition, you can also place small lights around your house to increase their output.

If you have a greenhouse, you need to remember that it will be very hot inside of it during the summer. That's why you might want to use an exhaust fan to help cool off your plants.

For beginners, try growing herbs and flowers in your greenhouse! You will save money when cooking because many herbs and flowers are expensive when bought from the market. It will also be much easier to grow them using a greenhouse compared to growing them outdoors.

Printed in Great Britain
by Amazon

60949314R00097